THIS BOOK BELONGS TO:

A CAREER GUIDE & PLANNER
FOR WOMEN LAWYERS WITH A LIFE

MARIANNE MERRITT TALBOT, ESQ.

Copyright 2020 by Marianne Merritt Talbot

All rights reserved. This book may not be reproduced in whole or in part, stored in a retrieval system, or transmitted in any form or by any means—electronic, mechanical, or other—without written permission from the publisher, except by a reviewer, who may quote brief passages in a review.

DISCLAIMER: This publication contains the opinions and ideas of its author. The advice contained herein is for informational purposes only. Every effort has been made to ensure the information contained in this book is complete and accurate.

ISBN: 978-1-7341988-1-2
Printed in the United States of America

Layout and design by Christy Y. Jenkins • seewhydesignworks.com

This book is dedicated to my
fierce and fabulous daughter,

BARBARA

Darling, may you never lose
that sparkle in your eyes.

Everything I do, I do for you.

Love,
Mommy

Praise for Balance

Marianne Talbot is not just an extraordinary coach, a longtime litigator, an excellent marketer and a full-time mother; she raises the game of everyone around her with her deep expertise, profound experiences and focus on what's really important. *Balance: A Planner for Women Lawyers With a Life* is a tool that synopsizes Marianne's life experience for the benefit of women lawyers everywhere who want to live a fuller and more balanced life. I recommend Marianne's book without hesitation.

—Jim Stapleton, Chief Marketing and Business Development Officer, Blank Rome LLP

Balance is an impressive and fun planner designed to help busy women lawyers achieve both their professional and personal goals. So often we are pulled in one direction and, in doing so, sacrifice some of the important things in our lives. With this simple planner, you can easily stay on track and achieve fulfillment while having fun. Wonderfully illustrated and easy to use, *Balance* will make a great gift for the busy lawyer in your life!

—Doreen Norden, Chief Marketing Officer, Becker & Poliakoff, P.A.

The *Balance* planner is both inspiring and practical for anyone who wants to effectively manage their time and become more organized while feeling engaged in the process and joyful about their goals! It is said that we suffer the cost for our bad habits in the future and Marianne's thoughtful tools and format will help anyone who wants to avoid that burden! I personally plan to use Balance and have recommended it to clients and friends.

—Kara Dodson, Executive Coach and Consultant, Volta Talent Strategies LLC

You'd be hard pressed to find a more passionate coach or a more detailed plan and approach to business development and life balance that what Marianne has presented in *Balance*. With wit, humor, and attention to detail on what's really important to women lawyers, you now have everything you need for quarterly, yearly, and long term success. I've personally witnessed lawyer transformation using Marianne's system. Follow her advice and in a short amount of time, you'll discover the balance and success you desire from your career.

—Cole Silver, Chief Client Officer, Blank Rome LLP

TABLE OF CONTENTS

INTRODUCTION 9

SUCCESS BY DESIGN: A SYSTEM THAT WORKS 10

BEFORE JUMPING IN 13

1ST QUARTER: WINTER 15
- Quarterly Review 16
  - January 20
  - February 32
  - March 44

2ND QUARTER: SPRING 57
- Quarterly Review 58
  - April 63
  - May 75
  - June 87

3RD QUARTER: SUMMER 99
- Quarterly Review 100
  - July 105
  - August 117
  - September 129

4TH QUARTER: AUTUMN 141
- Quarterly Review 142
  - October 147
  - November 159

CELEBRATE! HOLIDAY 171
    December 173

PERSONAL TOOLBOX 185
    Recommended Reading 186
    Creativity and Beauty 187
    Community and Connection. 188
    Decadence/Splurge 189
    Weekend Recharging 190
    Wellness and Movement 191
    Glowing Goddess Smoothie 192
    Rosé All Day? 193

PROFESSIONAL TOOLBOX 195
    BD Baby Steps 196
    Big Ticket Career Development 198
    Success Is a Team Sport 199
    Success Key: Personal Development 200
    Career Development Reading Resources 201
    Inner, Outer, and Professional Monthly Goals 202
    The French Macaron Theory 203

ACKNOWLEDGEMENTS 204

ABOUT MARIANNE 205

INTRODUCTION

Dearest Reader:

You, my dear, are a force of nature. There is no way you could have made it to this point in your career without possessing a fierce intelligence, disciplined drive, and the desire to live a vibrant and well-appointed life. Congratulations!

With all the pressures and responsibilities it takes to be a successful attorney, it may be difficult to focus on your personal goals and overall fierceness – and those wishes tend to take a back seat to office demands.

This planner condenses over 25 years of my experience as an attorney, coach, entrepreneur, professor, business development professional, and semi-professional pleasure-seeker. I have used the techniques in this book for clients, colleagues, audiences, mentees, and myself. I promise you they will work and will add more fun and success to your life – however you define them.

I hope this planner keeps you company on good days and bad – and that you find yourself feeling more balanced as a result of its use.

> *The future belongs to those who believe in the beauty of their dreams.*
> *– Eleanor Roosevelt*

With warmest wishes for your amazing success –

Success by Design: A System That Works

This planner lays out a system to help you create a year that surpasses your wildest expectations. The system is fun, simple, and effective. I am a connoisseur of **quick action** and **immediate gratification**, so this planner is designed to provide quick results through words, images, strategies, and resources.

The system is simple, with four related elements that work harmoniously together:
1. **SET GOALS:** identify them and write them down;
2. **TAKE ACTION:** design small and big steps to move towards your goals;
3. **NEVER STOP LEARNING:** pursue personal and professional excellence by devouring all you can on topics involving personal development, business success, and leadership; and
4. **HAVE FUN:** add more fun to your work and personal lives. Fun helps you think clearly, gives you energy, and increases your productivity in a joyful way.

This planner will hold your hand and walk you through your year – quarter by quarter, month by month, and week by week. It's chock-full of ideas and action steps, resources, and small bites of inspiration. You can use this planner methodically (suggested), or peruse the Toolboxes to get injections of energy and focus whenever you wish. However you decide to use this planner is absolutely perfect.

Planner Roadmap:

1. YOUR YEAR IN QUARTERS AND MONTHS

Each year tends to have its own rhythm, dictated in large part by seasonal plans, holidays, school calendars, and work deadlines. To that end, this planner is broken down by business quarter, season, month, and week to help guide your energy and projects as the year unfolds.

Each quarter begins with an intro note about the months ahead, followed by a Wheel of Life that will help you check in with eight different categories of your life (including career, fun, self-care, education, and sleep!). These wheels are a great tool to determine what areas of your life may want a little extra attention.

Next you'll find a checklist of career development strategies to consider implementing for the quarter, followed by a page that asks you to write down all of your personal and professional goals. The exercise of writing your goals down is important, so we provide you with lots of areas to do this throughout this book.

Each month has a focusing theme, as well as an area to identify your inner, outer, and professional goals. There is also a page to help you digest your month at its conclusion, as well as blank pages for notes and personal reflection.

2. YOUR YEAR IN WEEKS

The weekly planner spreads are the heart of the "balance" theme of this planner. They are unique in that they have two parts – a professional page as well as a personal page. Keeping track of both sides of your life as interdependent rather than in competition (where the personal side tends to come in last) will result in a happier, healthier, and more successful you.

3. BUSINESS DEVELOPMENT AND PERSONAL DEVELOPMENT

One of my favorite quotes is from Jim Rohn who said: "in order to have more, one must become more." This planner will help you do just that.

At the bottom of each planner page are 2 areas to check off as you go along – one for business development (aka "BD") (10 minutes a day) and personal development (30 minutes twice a week). Doing just 10 minutes of business development a day and 30 minutes of personal development a week (just one hour!) will create amazing results and will keep you inspired. And don't worry – I have lists of BD and personal development suggestions in the Toolboxes at the back of this book! These activities can involve reading, listening to podcasts or audiobooks while on your commute, or playing around on LinkedIn with a cup of coffee as you settle in at your desk each morning. Just plan on trying to do this each and every day and week, and notice the results and how this makes you feel. And don't forget to check those boxes at the bottom of your planner pages!

*Fill out your professional and personal pages the Friday before the week begins,
so when you arrive at your office the next workday, your week is organized and you'll be ready to go.*

4. GRATITUDE AND FABULOUSNESS

Each weekly planner spread has two areas in which to acknowledge yourself and your life: one for your week's gratitudes, and the other to document how fabulous you are. Add pieces to each as the week unfolds, and notice how doing this makes you feel.

Gratitude: Each gratitude block asks you to list what you are grateful for during that week. These could be big things or very small ones. The exercise of expressing gratitude decreases stress, reduces anxiety, improves sleep quality, makes you happier, and energetically opens the door to more good things in your life. Author Jack Canfield put it perfectly when he said, "Gratitude is the single most important ingredient to living a successful and fulfilled life."

Fabulousness: Yes, there is a box that asks you to acknowledge why you are fabulous! Here is where you make time to acknowledge yourself in ways big and small. Note: this box is not entitled: "Why I am Okay" or "Why I am Sufficient," because you are way more than that. Here is where you give yourself a pat on your own fine back. It can be that you won a big legal victory for a client or your company, you made it to the gym, woke up 30 minutes early to work on a side hustle, did some desk yoga, or helped a homeless woman by buying her a meal. Think about all the wonderful things you do in a week and I *know* you can find pieces that are pretty fabulous. Write them down and notice how that makes you feel.

TIP:

Be detailed about acknowledging yourself, because in some ways, this little corner can become a gorgeous little mini-journal of your life. I have clients who resisted this exercise and interestingly enough, the women who resisted it the most ended up being those who loved it the most.

5. TOOLBOXES:

I've included Personal and Professional Toolboxes that are full of ideas and strategies for your personal and professional goals, and that cover the various categories in your personal and professional pages. Some of them are:
- Career development activities that only take 10 minutes
- "Success as a Team Sport" – collaborating for professional success
- Personal development resources
- Recommended reading for instant elevation – as well as professional success
- Checklists with ideas for wellness, creativity, beauty, weekend recharging, community, how to pamper yourself, and more
- Inner, outer, and professional monthly goal ideas

Above all else, have using this journal! Mark it up, flag your favorite parts, add your own resources, write down your goals, dreams, and desires, and make it your own.

Before Jumping In: Set Your Goals

Before you dive into the pages of this planner, take a few minutes to write down some of your goals and desires. The entire aim of this book is for you to begin achieving those things in your life that you truly want. A key step (and a fun one) is to write down what they are.

This list isn't written in stone, and you can add (or remove) things whenever you want. This is *your* list. No one will see it. There are no grades or judgments. As you get used to identifying everything you *want*, it will become easier to identify additional things to add to your list.

Don't limit yourself to what you think you can get; think about what you want. Let your dreams run free. Some categories to contemplate:

- Places to visit
- People to meet
- Properties to own (ex. a mountain cabin, penthouse in the city, vineyard in France)
- Experiences you'd like to have (ex. skydiving, tattoo, start a family, run a marathon, write a book)
- Professions you'd like to explore (ex. acting, nonprofit work, sommelier, ballroom dancer, professor, bakery owner)
- Changes in your habits you'd like to make
- People you'd like to assist you (ex. nanny, personal trainer, executive coach, chauffeur, chef, etc.)
- Hobbies to start
- Friends you'd like to make
- Legendary love affairs you'd like to have
- Skills you wish to teach your children

Goals, Dreams, Desires:

I THINK EVERYTHING IN LIFE IS ART.
WHAT YOU DO. HOW YOU DRESS.
THE WAY YOU LOVE SOMEONE,
AND HOW YOU TALK.
YOUR SMILE AND YOUR PERSONALITY.
WHAT YOU BELIEVE IN,
AND ALL YOUR DREAMS.
THE WAY YOU DRINK YOUR TEA.
HOW YOU DECORATE YOUR HOME.
OR PARTY. YOUR GROCERY LIST.
THE FOOD YOU MAKE.
HOW YOUR WRITING LOOKS.
AND THE WAY YOU FEEL.
LIFE IS ART.

– HELENA BONHAM CARTER

1ST QUARTER
WINTER

1ST QUARTER
Planning Your Successful Year

Welcome to the first quarter of the year ("Q1"). In this introductory section, you are invited to evaluate areas of your life where you may need more balance – and what steps you want to put in play to create an amazing year. As in all areas of this book, we focus on both the personal and the professional.

First, using the Wheel of Life, think about where you feel you are in the categories identified. For those categories that are getting a particularly low score, identify action steps you can take to improve how you feel about them. This planner is full of ideas in all these areas; check out the "Personal Toolbox" for starters.

The second main section provides a structure and ideas of career development/business development actions that you can implement as this year begins. There are ideas for attorneys in firms, as well as ideas for attorneys who work as in-house counsel, at nonprofits, and in the government. For those ideas that don't directly apply to where you are practicing, think how you may be able to tweak them to apply to you. What can you easily jump on, and what more ambitious goals speak to you? Mark the ones you like most and add them to the first week planner pages in January. Refer back to the checklists regularly and continue building on your successes in your weekly worksheets.

Third, write your personal and professional goals for the next 3 months on the page provided – and include everything you noted in the Wheel of Life, the goal section in the introduction, and any other checklists in this planner. Look at this list regularly and edit it as you see fit! It's your list – have fun with it. Every time you complete or achieve a goal, put a check mark next to the achieved goals and give yourself a round of applause.

Think big, bold, and new.

Freedom lies in being bold.
— Robert Frost

Q1 Wheel of Life

This quarterly Wheel of Life is designed to have you honestly assess where you are, and where you need support, in each area.

ASSESSMENT:
On a scale of 0 (low) to 10 (high), where do you feel you are in each area? Mark that score on the Wheel.

REFLECTION:
What areas do you feel most need more attention, focus, resources, and support?

DESIGN:
For each area you feel needs more attention, design three action steps you will take to support this goal. What supports can you add? What pieces of your life can you simplify to focus attention on areas that want it?

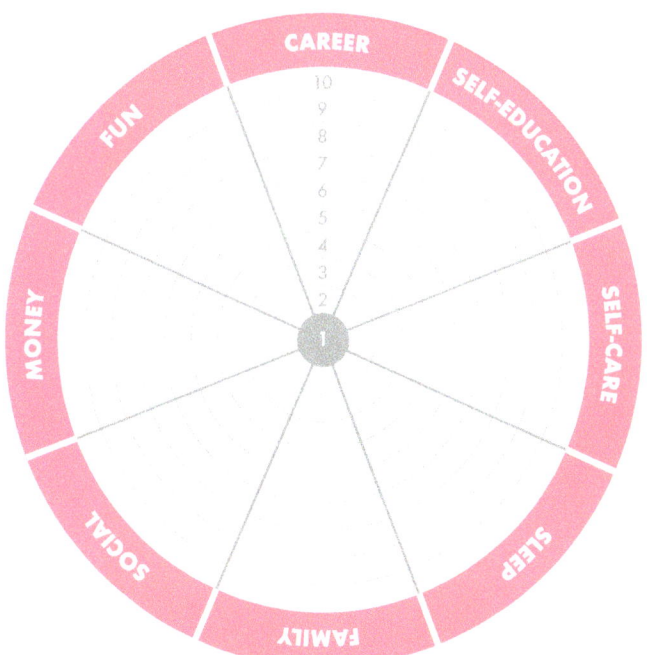

AREA: _____

Action Steps:

1.

2.

3.

AREA: _____

Action Steps:

1.

2.

3.

AREA: _____

Action Steps:

1.

2.

3.

Q1 CAREER DEVELOPMENT STRATEGIES

- ROI (Return on Investment) Review and Recap: what worked and what didn't last year? What was fun (or not)? What can you do differently?

- Study the industry that your organization or law firm clients are in, and stay abreast of cutting-edge topics that may impact them. Become the "go to" person related to trends in your industry.

- Identify at least 10 potential clients, fellow general counsel/in-house counsel, or other professional peers, that you want to connect with this quarter. Write the list down and aim to connect with one per quarter.

- Attend at least one trade organization, bar association, or networking meeting per month. Volunteer for leadership in those organizations you like most.

- Identify one hot topic and research to focus your legal business development and thought leadership efforts.

- Send thank you cards to any clients whose work you completed.

- Decide what thought leadership activities you should do: articles, CLEs, lectures, etc.

- Reach out to a CLE provider (or internally at your firm or company) to propose CLE programs for the year. They need at least 30 days' notice to provide accreditation, so come up with ideas and any co-presenters, and then pitch the program to them.

- Go onsite with a client or invite outside counsel to your office to review work, meet management and employees, see facilities, socialize, and discuss additional concerns.

- Schedule one complimentary client/prospect presentation per quarter (per month if you have the ability) – either onsite at their location, or at your office (or team up with a complementary practice area for extra exposure).

- Write one blog post per month and distribute widely to your networks.

- Read (or listen to) one book per month on how to develop your business development or sales skills.

- Identify the calendar of – and pursue – local, regional, and national rankings and awards. Add their deadlines to your calendar and begin preparing lists of cases and client references, and engage partner support as necessary.

- Schedule a festive New Year happy hour for clients/referral sources/non-lawyer colleagues at your office or off-site (whether or not you pay for the event, it's fun to organize and perhaps you can pay for one round or the like – it should not break the bank).

- Send follow-up "thank you" or holiday notes to anyone who sent you a card, gift, or other holiday salutations.

- Congratulations on all the steps you are taking to build a fabulous year!

Q1 Professional Goals

Q1 Personal Goals

And suddenly you know: It's time to start something new and trust in the magic of new beginnings.
— MEISTER ECKHART

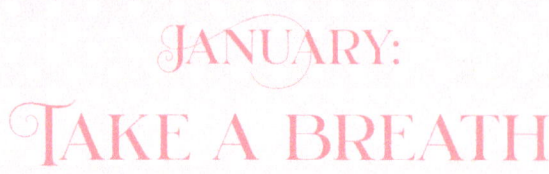

January: Take a Breath

With the holidays behind us, January – with its long days and low energy – gives us space to take a breath, reflect on the successes and challenges of last year, and set our intentions for this new chapter. Take a few minutes to think about:

- What do I need to happen this year?
- What do I *want* to happen this year?

Consider things that you no longer need in your life – including in physical spaces like your office or home. What can you release or simplify – things, habits, even people. Spend some time tidying up your spaces, discarding or donating anything that does not "spark joy" (using the Marie Kondo standard), and reflect on how giving things away may help you gain more clarity (and is pleasing to the eye, to boot).

In these darker days, deliberately slow down. Read for pleasure. Wrap yourself in cozy blankets. Make hot chocolate. Take naps. Give yourself permission to slow down.

Inner Goal

Outer Goal

Professional Goal

Life is not measured by the number of breaths we take, but by the moments that take our breath away.
— Anonymous

SUNDAY	MONDAY	TUESDAY	WEDNESDAY	THURSDAY	FRIDAY	SATURDAY

This Week's Goals:

WEEK OF _____

Highest Priority Work Activities

Long-term Projects To Keep An Eye On

Career/Business/Personal Development

Connecting/Networking

Miscellaneous

10 Minute BD Checklist:

☐ M ☐ T ☐ W ☐ TH ☐ F

Happy New Year!

This Week's Gratitudes:

Weekend Recharging

Community & Connection

Pleasure Reading

Creativity & Beauty

Decadence/Splurge

Wellness & Movement

Appointments & Tasks

Companion Care/Other

Custom Category: _____

30 Minutes of Personal Development 2x Week:
☐ ☐

Why I Am Fabulous:

This Week's Goals:

WEEK OF _____

Highest Priority Work Activities

Long-term Projects To Keep An Eye On

Career/Business/Personal Development

Connecting/Networking

Miscellaneous

10 Minute BD Checklist:

☐ M ☐ T ☐ W ☐ TH ☐ F

This Week's Gratitudes:

Weekend Recharging

Pleasure Reading

Decadence/Splurge

Appointments & Tasks

Companion Care/Other

Custom Category: _____

30 Minutes of Personal Development 2x Week:
☐ ☐

Community & Connection

Creativity & Beauty

Wellness & Movement

Why I Am Fabulous:

This Week's Goals:

WEEK OF _____

Highest Priority Work Activities

Long-term Projects To Keep An Eye On

Career/Business/Personal Development

Connecting/Networking

Miscellaneous

10 Minute BD Checklist:

☐ M ☐ T ☐ W ☐ TH ☐ F

This Week's Gratitudes:

Weekend Recharging

Pleasure Reading

Decadence/Splurge

Appointments & Tasks

Companion Care/Other

Custom Category: _____

30 Minutes of Personal Development 2x Week:
☐ ☐

Community & Connection

Creativity & Beauty

Wellness & Movement

Why I Am Fabulous:

This Week's Goals:

WEEK OF _____

Highest Priority Work Activities

Long-term Projects To Keep An Eye On

Career/Business/Personal Development

Connecting/Networking

Miscellaneous

10 Minute BD Checklist:

☐ M ☐ T ☐ W ☐ TH ☐ F

This Week's Gratitudes:

Weekend Recharging

Pleasure Reading

Decadence/Splurge

Appointments & Tasks

Companion Care/Other

Custom Category: _____

30 Minutes of Personal Development 2x Week:
☐ ☐

Community & Connection

Creativity & Beauty

Wellness & Movement

Why I Am Fabulous:

WHEN YOU SAY "NO" TO SOMETHING YOU
DON'T WANT TO DO, YOU SAY "YES" TO YOU.

Tie a Bow Around January

Things I Did Well

Challenges I Encountered

What I Am Grateful For This Month

FEBRUARY: THINK PINK

With the days becoming longer, February has more energy in the air, and there's a sense that the heaviness of winter is beginning to lift. February is also a month that asks us to spread additional love – to others as well as ourselves. Pink – often a color linked to February, particularly because of Valentine's Day – is a color of caring, compassion, hope, and love. If you love this color as much as I do, add some splashes to your office, home, and wardrobe.

What ways can you show yourself more self-care, self-love, and self-respect? Are there habits you might like to add, and others to release? Are you overdue for a massage, doctor's appointment, or other self-care?

Do you want to shower others in your life with extra love? Spend some time writing letters (a lost art), making phone calls (leave special voice messages if you don't reach them in person), and reconnecting. The inimitable chef and television personality Julia Child and her husband Paul would forgo traditional holiday cards and would instead send Valentine's Day cards to their friends and family. Is this a tradition you might also want to start for yourself?

Inner Goal

Outer Goal

Professional Goal

If I'd observed all the rules, I'd never have got anywhere.
—MARILYN MONROE

Month at a Glance

SUNDAY	MONDAY	TUESDAY	WEDNESDAY	THURSDAY	FRIDAY	SATURDAY

This Week's Goals:

WEEK OF _____

Highest Priority Work Activities

Long-term Projects To Keep An Eye On

Career/Business/Personal Development

Connecting/Networking

Miscellaneous

10 Minute BD Checklist:

☐ M ☐ T ☐ W ☐ TH ☐ F

This Week's Gratitudes:

Weekend Recharging

Community & Connection

Pleasure Reading

Creativity & Beauty

Decadence/Splurge

Wellness & Movement

Appointments & Tasks

Companion Care/Other

Custom Category: _____

30 Minutes of Personal Development 2x Week:
☐ ☐

Why I Am Fabulous:

This Week's Goals:

WEEK OF _____

Highest Priority Work Activities

Long-term Projects To Keep An Eye On

Career/Business/Personal Development

Connecting/Networking

Miscellaneous

10 Minute BD Checklist:

❏ M ❏ T ❏ W ❏ TH ❏ F

This Week's Gratitudes:

Weekend Recharging

Pleasure Reading

Decadence/Splurge

Appointments & Tasks

Companion Care/Other

Custom Category: _____

30 Minutes of Personal Development 2x Week:
☐ ☐

Community & Connection

Creativity & Beauty

Wellness & Movement

Why I Am Fabulous:

This Week's Goals:

WEEK OF _____

Highest Priority Work Activities

Long-term Projects To Keep An Eye On

Career/Business/Personal Development

Connecting/Networking

Miscellaneous

10 Minute BD Checklist:

☐ M ☐ T ☐ W ☐ TH ☐ F

This Week's Gratitudes:

Weekend Recharging

Pleasure Reading

Decadence/Splurge

Appointments & Tasks

Companion Care/Other

Custom Category: _____

30 Minutes of Personal Development 2x Week:
☐ ☐

Community & Connection

Creativity & Beauty

Wellness & Movement

Why I Am Fabulous:

This Week's Goals:

WEEK OF _____

Highest Priority Work Activities

Long-term Projects To Keep An Eye On

Career/Business/Personal Development

Connecting/Networking

Miscellaneous

SLEEP MORE

10 Minute BD Checklist:

❏ M ❏ T ❏ W ❏ TH ❏ F

This Week's Gratitudes:

Weekend Recharging

Pleasure Reading

Decadence/Splurge

Appointments & Tasks

Companion Care/Other

Custom Category: _____

30 Minutes of Personal Development 2x Week:
☐ ☐

Community & Connection

Creativity & Beauty

Wellness & Movement

Why I Am Fabulous:

NOTES

"I BELIEVE IN PINK. I BELIEVE THAT LAUGHING IS THE BEST CALORIE BURNER. I BELIEVE IN KISSING, KISSING A LOT. I BELIEVE IN BEING STRONG WHEN EVERYTHING SEEMS TO BE GOING WRONG. I BELIEVE THAT HAPPY GIRLS ARE THE PRETTIEST GIRLS. I BELIEVE THAT TOMORROW IS ANOTHER DAY AND I BELIEVE IN MIRACLES."

— AUDREY HEPBURN

Tie A Bow Around February

Things I Did Well

Challenges I Encountered

What I Am Grateful For This Month

MARCH: PLANT SEEDS

March 20 (or thereabouts) is the official start of spring. This month asks you to plant seeds that can result in wonderful blossoms. Consider visualizing your life as a garden – what is planted in each section? What areas need more tending? Maybe your weekends are lavender, your career section peppermint, personal life a row of bright yellow roses, creative life a bed of colorful wildflowers. What else might you like to plant?

Are there big or small projects that you haven't yet paid attention to, in your personal or professional lives? Look over your goal lists and all the ideas in this book and see what jumps out at you.

As the first quarter of the year concludes, plan a special occasion – a fancy dinner out, or a cozy potluck in with friends – to celebrate each other, and all you are creating.

Inner Goal

Outer Goal

Professional Goal

Show me your garden, and I will tell you what you are.
ALFRED AUSTIN

Month at a Glance

SUNDAY	MONDAY	TUESDAY	WEDNESDAY	THURSDAY	FRIDAY	SATURDAY

This Week's Goals:

WEEK OF _____

Highest Priority Work Activities

Long-term Projects To Keep An Eye On

Career/Business/Personal Development

Connecting/Networking

Miscellaneous

10 Minute BD Checklist:

☐ M ☐ T ☐ W ☐ TH ☐ F

This Week's Gratitudes:

Weekend Recharging

Pleasure Reading

Decadence/Splurge

Appointments & Tasks

Companion Care/Other

Custom Category: _____

30 Minutes of Personal Development 2x Week:
☐ ☐

Community & Connection

Creativity & Beauty

Wellness & Movement

Why I Am Fabulous:

This Week's Goals:

WEEK OF _____

Highest Priority Work Activities

Long-term Projects To Keep An Eye On

Career/Business/Personal Development

Connecting/Networking

Miscellaneous

10 Minute BD Checklist:

☐ M   ☐ T   ☐ W   ☐ TH   ☐ F

This Week's Gratitudes:

Weekend Recharging

Pleasure Reading

Decadence/Splurge

Appointments & Tasks

Companion Care/Other

Custom Category: _____

30 Minutes of Personal Development 2x Week:
☐ ☐

Community & Connection

Creativity & Beauty

Wellness & Movement

Why I Am Fabulous:

This Week's Goals:

WEEK OF _____

Highest Priority Work Activities

Long-term Projects To Keep An Eye On

Career/Business/Personal Development

Connecting/Networking

Miscellaneous

10 Minute BD Checklist:

☐ M ☐ T ☐ W ☐ TH ☐ F

This Week's Gratitudes:

Weekend Recharging

Community & Connection

Pleasure Reading

Creativity & Beauty

Decadence/Splurge

Wellness & Movement

Appointments & Tasks

Companion Care/Other

Why I Am Fabulous:

Custom Category: _____

30 Minutes of Personal Development 2x Week:
☐ ☐

This Week's Goals:

WEEK OF _____

Highest Priority Work Activities

Long-term Projects To Keep An Eye On

Career/Business/Personal Development

Connecting/Networking

Miscellaneous

She believed she could so she did

10 Minute BD Checklist:

☐ M ☐ T ☐ W ☐ TH ☐ F

This Week's Gratitudes:

Weekend Recharging

Pleasure Reading

Decadence/Splurge

Appointments & Tasks

Companion Care/Other

Custom Category: _____

30 Minutes of Personal Development 2x Week:
☐ ☐

Community & Connection

Creativity & Beauty

Wellness & Movement

Why I Am Fabulous:

AMAZING NEW DOORS OPEN FOR YOU EVERY DAY.

Tie a Bow Around March

Things I Did Well

Challenges I Encountered

What I Am Grateful For This Month

Revive your light.
Manifest your dreams. Know your worth.
– Alex Elle

2ND QUARTER
Spring

2ND QUARTER
Spring Into Action

Welcome to the next quarter of the year! How did Q1 go? What worked? What didn't? What might you fine-tune or change? Congratulations on moving in the direction of your success, in big steps and small. How did it feel to try new strategies?

Now, once again, check in with yourself using this Wheel of Life and the career development success strategies. Where did you have movement? What may have not moved as much as you might like? Revisit the action steps you were planning to take – what will you keep doing? Need to add anything else? If three areas of focus are too overwhelming, just choose one and devote some of your genius ideas and energy to it. It's all perfect. Just get into action.

Don't forget to write down your goals! Writing them down helps them manifest much more quickly (don't ask me how, but it does). Include the goals you identified last quarter that you want to take along, drop the ones that no longer speak to you or you achieved, and add all your new ones.

Have fun with this. There is no right or wrong. The fact you're checking in with yourself is more than most human beings do. Celebrate yourself and the steps you are taking in the direction of your dreams.

Dreams don't work unless you do.

Q2 Wheel of Life

This quarterly Wheel of Life is designed to have you honestly assess where you are, and where you need support, in each area.

ASSESSMENT:
On a scale of 0 (low) to 10 (high), where do you feel you are in each area? Mark that score on the Wheel.

REFLECTION:
What areas do you feel most need more attention, focus, resources, and support?

DESIGN:
For each area you feel needs more attention, design three action steps you will take to support this goal. What supports can you add? What pieces of your life can you simplify to focus attention on areas that want it?

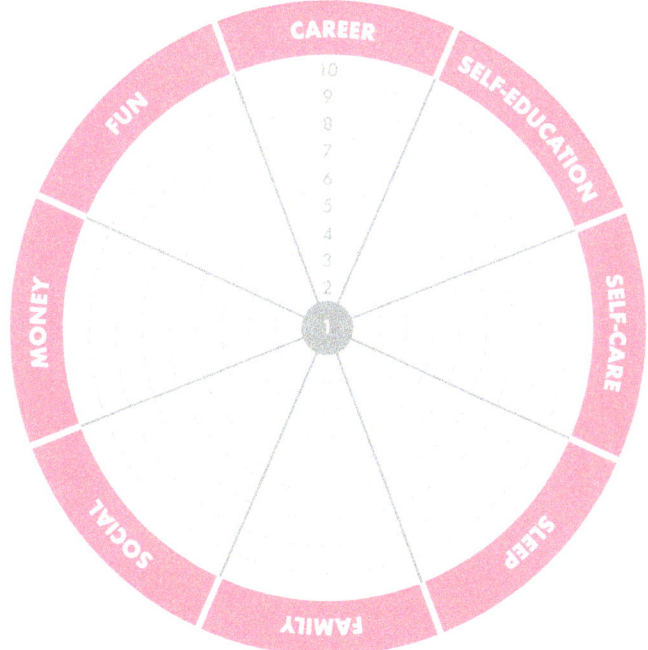

AREA: _____

Action Steps:

1.

2.

3.

AREA: _____

Action Steps:

1.

2.

3.

AREA: _____

Action Steps:

1.

2.

3.

Q2 Career Development Strategies

- Review Q1 plans – did you hit your goals? Why or why not? What additional supports might you need to complete them?

- For any of the hot topics you identified in Q1, reach out to reporter (local, regional, or national) to offer to write an article on the piece. Continue doing this during the year – and build relationships with those reporters.

Your Ideas:

- Begin planning a vacation break. Rest is important to your success.

- Identify at least 10 potential clients, fellow general counsel/in-house counsel, or other professional peers, that you want to connect with this quarter. Write the list down and aim to connect with one per quarter.

- Attend at least one trade organization, bar association, or networking meeting per month.

- Schedule one complimentary client/prospect presentation (ongoing).

- Write one blog post per month and distribute widely to your networks.

- Read one business development or business skills book.

- Send thank you, birthday and other cards (ongoing).

- Schedule a spring happy hour for clients/referral sources/non-lawyer colleagues at your office or off-site.

- Send thank you cards to any clients whose work you completed.

- Go onsite with a client or invite outside counsel to your office to review work, meet management and employees, see facilities, socialize, and discuss additional concerns.

- Congratulate yourself on the business development muscles you are flexing!

Q2 Professional Goals

Q2 Personal Goals

To love oneself is the beginning of a life-long romance.
— Oscar Wilde

April: Revive

In this first full month of spring, the world is being reborn, and you are too. Move your body in new ways and try new activities – even simply taking a new walking route to the office. And add some spice to your life – perhaps consider trying a new food every day. Mix things up, shake up your routine in small ways – or big.

This is also the beginning of the second quarter of your career development initiatives this year – what achievements did you have in Q1, and what projects are you following up on? What worked? What can you add to your current efforts?

Inner Goal

Outer Goal

Professional Goal

And the day came that the risk to remain tight in a bud was more painful than the risk it took to blossom.
— Anaïs Nin

SUNDAY	MONDAY	TUESDAY	WEDNESDAY	THURSDAY	FRIDAY	SATURDAY

This Week's Goals:

WEEK OF _____

Highest Priority Work Activities

Long-term Projects To Keep An Eye On

Career/Business/Personal Development

Connecting/Networking

Miscellaneous

10 Minute BD Checklist:

☐ M ☐ T ☐ W ☐ TH ☐ F

This Week's Gratitudes:

Weekend Recharging

Community & Connection

Pleasure Reading

Creativity & Beauty

Decadence/Splurge

Wellness & Movement

Appointments & Tasks

Companion Care/Other

Custom Category: _____

30 Minutes of Personal Development 2x Week:
☐ ☐

Why I Am Fabulous:

This Week's Goals:

WEEK OF _____

Highest Priority Work Activities

Long-term Projects To Keep An Eye On

Career/Business/Personal Development

Connecting/Networking

Miscellaneous

10 Minute BD Checklist:

❏ M ❏ T ❏ W ❏ TH ❏ F

This Week's Gratitudes:

Weekend Recharging

Pleasure Reading

Decadence/Splurge

Appointments & Tasks

Companion Care/Other

Custom Category: _____

30 Minutes of Personal Development 2x Week:
☐ ☐

Community & Connection

Creativity & Beauty

Wellness & Movement

Why I am Fabulous:

This Week's Goals:

WEEK OF _____

Highest Priority Work Activities

Long-term Projects To Keep An Eye On

Career/Business/Personal Development

Connecting/Networking

Miscellaneous

10 Minute BD Checklist:

☐ M ☐ T ☐ W ☐ TH ☐ F

This Week's Gratitudes:

Weekend Recharging

Pleasure Reading

Decadence/Splurge

Appointments & Tasks

Companion Care/Other

Custom Category: _____

30 Minutes of Personal Development 2x Week:
☐ ☐

Community & Connection

Creativity & Beauty

Wellness & Movement

Why I am Fabulous:

This Week's Goals:

WEEK OF _____

Highest Priority Work Activities

Long-term Projects To Keep An Eye On

Career/Business/Personal Development

Connecting/Networking

Miscellaneous

10 Minute BD Checklist

☐ M ☐ T ☐ W ☐ TH ☐ F

This Week's Gratitudes:

Weekend Recharging

Pleasure Reading

Decadence/Splurge

Appointments & Tasks

Companion Care/Other

Custom Category: _____

30 Minutes of Personal Development 2x Week:
☐ ☐

Community & Connection

Creativity & Beauty

Wellness & Movement

Why I Am Fabulous:

Pour yourself a drink,
put on some lipstick and pull yourself together.
— Elizabeth Taylor

Tie a Bow Around April

Things I Did Well

Challenges I Encountered

What I Am Grateful For This Month

MAY: CONFIDENCE

Congratulations on trying new things and building new personal and professional muscles. With the acquisition of new skills may come the feeling of new confidence. Where do you feel more confident in your life? Are there areas you feel you shrink back, thinking you're not quite ready for prime time? Consider researching new ways and means to build those skills and practice them (check out the numerous resources in this book). Even taking one hour this week to do some new self-education may help you realize new breakthroughs are within your grasp.

The birth stone for the month of May is the regal green emerald, which symbolizes royalty, wit, eloquence, and foresight. Cleopatra herself reportedly adorned herself and her palace with emeralds and gifted them to visiting dignitaries as a sign of her wealth and power. That image of Cleopatra confidently adorned with jewels has captivated humanity for centuries. The definition of "adorn" includes "to enliven or decorate" and "to add beauty to." Play around with the concept of adornment this month, as it applies to you, your office, your home, even your car. What might adorning yourself look like? Notice how adorning yourself – even just a little – makes you feel.

Inner Goal

Outer Goal

Professional Goal

YOU ARE NOT HERE TO SHRINK DOWN TO LESS, BUT TO BLOSSOM INTO MORE OF WHO YOU REALLY ARE.

OPRAH WINFREY

SUNDAY	MONDAY	TUESDAY	WEDNESDAY	THURSDAY	FRIDAY	SATURDAY

THIS WEEK'S GOALS:

WEEK OF _____

Highest Priority Work Activities

Long-term Projects To Keep An Eye On

Career/Business/Personal Development

Connecting/Networking

Miscellaneous

10 MINUTE BD CHECKLIST:

❏ M ❏ T ❏ W ❏ TH ❏ F

This Week's Gratitudes:

Weekend Recharging

Pleasure Reading

Decadence/Splurge

Appointments & Tasks

Companion Care/Other

Custom Category: _____

30 Minutes of Personal Development 2x Week:
☐ ☐

Community & Connection

Creativity & Beauty

Wellness & Movement

Why I Am Fabulous:

This Week's Goals:

WEEK OF _____

Highest Priority Work Activities

Long-term Projects To Keep An Eye On

Career/Business/Personal Development

Connecting/Networking

Miscellaneous

10 Minute BD Checklist:

☐ M ☐ T ☐ W ☐ TH ☐ F

This Week's Gratitudes:

Weekend Recharging

Community & Connection

Pleasure Reading

Creativity & Beauty

Decadence/Splurge

Wellness & Movement

Appointments & Tasks

Companion Care/Other

Why I Am Fabulous:

Custom Category: _____

30 Minutes of Personal Development 2x Week:
☐ ☐

This Week's Goals:

WEEK OF _____

Highest Priority Work Activities

Long-term Projects To Keep An Eye On

Career/Business/Personal Development

Connecting/Networking

Miscellaneous

10 Minute BD Checklist:

☐ M ☐ T ☐ W ☐ TH ☐ F

This Week's Gratitudes:

Weekend Recharging

Pleasure Reading

Decadence/Splurge

Appointments & Tasks

Companion Care/Other

Custom Category: _____

30 Minutes of Personal Development 2x Week:
☐ ☐

Community & Connection

Creativity & Beauty

Wellness & Movement

Why I Am Fabulous:

This Week's Goals:

WEEK OF _____

Highest Priority Work Activities

Long-term Projects To Keep An Eye On

Career/Business/Personal Development

Connecting/Networking

Miscellaneous

10 Minute BD Checklist:

☐ M ☐ T ☐ W ☐ TH ☐ F

This Week's Gratitudes:

Weekend Recharging

Pleasure Reading

Decadence/Splurge

Appointments & Tasks

Companion Care/Other

Custom Category: _____

30 Minutes of Personal Development 2x Week:
☐ ☐

Community & Connection

Creativity & Beauty

Wellness & Movement

Why I Am Fabulous:

Inaction breeds doubt and fear. Action breeds confidence and courage. If you want to conquer fear, do not sit home and think about it. Go out and get busy.
— Dale Carnegie

Tie a Bow Around May

Things I Did Well

Challenges I Encountered

What I Am Grateful For This Month

JUNE: STOP AND SMELL THE ROSES

In Greek mythology, the feminine rose was associated with Aphrodite, the goddess of love, beauty, and pleasure. The ancient Greeks knew how to appreciate these special blooms, using rose petals to perfume their baths and sprinkle on floors to honor notable guests who would tread upon them. The scent of roses is considered an anti-depressant and anti-anxiety treatment, and is at the heart of innumerable fragrances. In modern times, yellow roses symbolize friendship; white roses new beginnings; pink roses, grace, happiness and admiration; and red roses, passion and romance. If you were a rose, what colors might you be?

One key to raising beautiful roses is the special love and care you must show them. Is there anything about the process of raising roses that might be applicable to your own life? Is there a place that needs some weeding? Or is there a place that needs some gentle tending, kind words, and a smidge of extra water? Find those spots and embrace them with extra TLC.

While you are at it, keep some fresh roses on your desk this month, and notice how doing so makes you feel. Perhaps leave a surprise bouquet on a colleague's desk who you know is going through a hard time. And when they start wilting, scatter some on a table where you've set a celebratory meal to congratulate yourself for all the steps you took in Q2. Or do your own special petal toss – just for you!

Inner Goal

Outer Goal

Professional Goal

It is the time you have spent on your rose that makes her so important.
ANTOINE DE SAINT-EXUPERY, "THE LITTLE PRINCE"

Month at a Glance

SUNDAY	MONDAY	TUESDAY	WEDNESDAY	THURSDAY	FRIDAY	SATURDAY

This Week's Goals:

WEEK OF _____

Highest Priority Work Activities

Long-term Projects To Keep An Eye On

Career/Business/Personal Development

Connecting/Networking

Miscellaneous

10 Minute BD Checklist:

❏ M ❏ T ❏ W ❏ TH ❏ F

This Week's Gratitudes:

Weekend Recharging

Pleasure Reading

Decadence/Splurge

Appointments & Tasks

Companion Care/Other

Custom Category: _____

30 Minutes of Personal Development 2x Week:
☐ ☐

Community & Connection

Creativity & Beauty

Wellness & Movement

Why I Am Fabulous:

This Week's Goals:

WEEK OF _____

Highest Priority Work Activities

Long-term Projects To Keep An Eye On

Career/Business/Personal Development

Connecting/Networking

Miscellaneous

10 Minute BD Checklist:

☐ M   ☐ T   ☐ W   ☐ TH   ☐ F

This Week's Gratitudes:

Weekend Recharging

Pleasure Reading

Decadence/Splurge

Appointments & Tasks

Companion Care/Other

Custom Category: _____

30 Minutes of Personal Development 2x Week:
☐ ☐

Community & Connection

Creativity & Beauty

Wellness & Movement

Why I Am Fabulous:

This Week's Goals:

WEEK OF _____

Highest Priority Work Activities

Long-term Projects To Keep An Eye On

Career/Business/Personal Development

Connecting/Networking

Miscellaneous

10 Minute BD Checklist:

❏ M ❏ T ❏ W ❏ TH ❏ F

This Week's Gratitudes:

Weekend Recharging

Pleasure Reading

Decadence/Splurge

Appointments & Tasks

Companion Care/Other

Custom Category: _____

30 Minutes of Personal Development 2x Week:
❏ ❏

Community & Connection

Creativity & Beauty

Wellness & Movement

Why I Am Fabulous:

This Week's Goals:

WEEK OF _____

Highest Priority Work Activities

Long-term Projects To Keep An Eye On

Career/Business/Personal Development

Connecting/Networking

Miscellaneous

10 Minute BD Checklist:

☐ M   ☐ T   ☐ W   ☐ TH   ☐ F

This Week's Gratitudes:

Weekend Recharging

Pleasure Reading

Decadence/Splurge

Appointments & Tasks

Companion Care/Other

Custom Category: _____

30 Minutes of Personal Development 2x Week:
☐ ☐

Community & Connection

Creativity & Beauty

Wellness & Movement

Why I Am Fabulous:

JUST ADD GLITTER.

Tie A Bow Around June

Things I Did Well

Challenges I Encountered

What I Am Grateful For This Month

Notes

> Twenty years from now you will be more disappointed by the things that you didn't do than by the ones you did do. So throw off the bowlines, sail away from safe harbor, catch the trade winds in your sails. Explore. Dream. Discover.
> — Mark Twain

3RD QUARTER
SUMMER

3RD QUARTER
CONTINUE GROWING

A main piece of this planner asks you to work on your personal development. How is that going? Do you feel new muscles (figurative and literal) growing in your mind and body?

In Q3, you are asked to keep growing. Keep moving. Continue the momentum. Stopped to rest for a little while? That's okay— but pick up your fabulous bag and continue moving forward soon.

Look at your professional goals in particular and see if you are positioned to complete the successes you want for this year. Did you write any articles or blog posts yet this year? Organize any speaking engagements? Regularly attend any networking/industry events (particularly any that are not legal industry-related)? Take clients, prospects, or referral sources to breakfast or lunch?

If not, keep growing. Do what you were intending to when you started this process. Discipline is the key here — apply consistent self-discipline to continue growing and expanding your skills, influence, success, and happiness.

> IF EVERYTHING WAS PERFECT,
> YOU WOULD NEVER LEARN
> AND YOU WOULD NEVER GROW.
> — BEYONCE

Q3 Wheel of Life

This quarterly Wheel of Life is designed to have you honestly assess where you are, and where you need support, in each area.

ASSESSMENT:
On a scale of 0 (low) to 10 (high), where do you feel you are in each area? Mark that score on the Wheel.

REFLECTION:
What areas do you feel most need more attention, focus, resources, and support?

DESIGN:
For each area you feel needs more attention, design three action steps you will take to support this goal. What supports can you add? What pieces of your life can you simplify to focus attention on areas that want it?

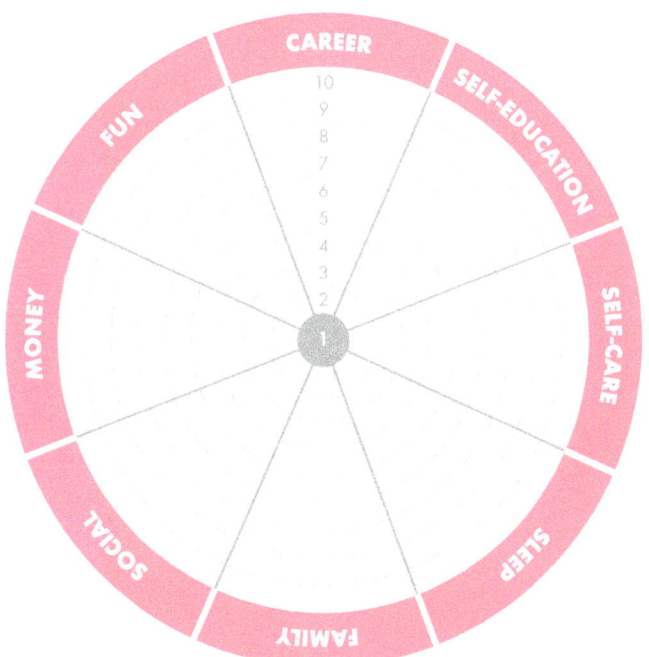

AREA: _____

Action Steps:

1.

2.

3.

AREA: _____

Action Steps:

1.

2.

3.

AREA: _____

Action Steps:

1.

2.

3.

Q3 Career Development Strategies

- Review Winter and Spring lists above. Review Q1 and Q2 plans – did you hit your goals? Try to complete any pieces you didn't do.

- Identify at least 10 potential clients, fellow general counsel/in-house counsel, or other professional peers, that you want to connect with this quarter. Write the list down and aim to connect with one per quarter.

- Think about and start planning a pro bono or non-profit fund-raising project that your firm, company, or organization can help support in the fall. Take the lead in planning, inviting co-sponsors, and publicizing the event, and be sure to promote your leadership in the project with your supervisors and colleagues (toot your own horn!).

- Write one blog post per month and distribute widely to your networks.

- Schedule one complimentary client/prospect presentation per quarter (ongoing).

- Send thank you, birthday, and other cards (ongoing).

- Attend at least one trade organization, bar association, or networking meeting per month.

- Schedule a relaxed summer happy hour for clients/referral sources/non-lawyer colleagues at your office or off-site.

- Send thank you cards to any clients whose work you completed.

- Go onsite with a client or invite outside counsel to your office to review work, meet management and employees, see facilities, socialize, and discuss additional concerns.

- Plan some time to relax, you deserve it!

Q3 Professional Goals

Q3 Personal Goals

I am not lucky. You know what I am? I am smart. I am talented. I take advantage of the opportunities that come my way and I work really, really hard. Don't call me lucky. Call me a badass.

— SHONDA RHIMES

JULY:
FREEDOM

Remember the feeling of anticipation and joy when school let out for the summer? As the days counted down to the end of the year, you could hardly pay attention to lessons as your mind was filled with thoughts of your impending freedom.

We can recapture those days of long ago, even if we spend most of our time in the office. You can do this by tapping into your inner child and thinking about what you used to love to do – was it dancing, drawing, skipping, playing ball, jumping in puddles? Build in small activities to revisit those days – grab an ice cream cone on the way home, put a sprinkler in your back yard, take a walk in the summer rain (sans umbrella), take in a double-feature on the weekend with an extra-big bucket of popcorn. What are small things – or large – that you can do with yourself, friends, and family, that makes you feel free?

Inner Goal

Outer Goal

Professional Goal

I KNEW WHEN I MET YOU AN ADVENTURE WAS GOING TO HAPPEN.
A.A. MILNE, WINNIE THE POOH

Month at a Glance

SUNDAY	MONDAY	TUESDAY	WEDNESDAY	THURSDAY	FRIDAY	SATURDAY

THIS WEEK'S GOALS:

WEEK OF _____

Highest Priority Work Activities

Long-term Projects To Keep An Eye On

Career/Business/Personal Development

Connecting/Networking

Miscellaneous

10 MINUTE BD CHECKLIST:

❏ M ❏ T ❏ W ❏ TH ❏ F

This Week's Gratitudes:

Weekend Recharging

Community & Connection

Pleasure Reading

Creativity & Beauty

Decadence/Splurge

Wellness & Movement

Appointments & Tasks

Companion Care/Other

Custom Category: _____

30 Minutes of Personal Development 2x Week:
☐ ☐

Why I Am Fabulous:

THIS WEEK'S GOALS:

WEEK OF _____

Highest Priority Work Activities

Long-term Projects To Keep An Eye On

Career/Business/Personal Development

Connecting/Networking

Miscellaneous

10 MINUTE BD CHECKLIST:

❏ M ❏ T ❏ W ❏ TH ❏ F

This Week's Gratitudes:

Weekend Recharging

Pleasure Reading

Decadence/Splurge

Appointments & Tasks

Companion Care/Other

Custom Category: _____

30 Minutes of Personal Development 2x Week:
❑ ❑

Community & Connection

Creativity & Beauty

Wellness & Movement

Why I Am Fabulous:

This Week's Goals:

WEEK OF _____

Highest Priority Work Activities

Long-term Projects To Keep An Eye On

Career/Business/Personal Development

Connecting/Networking

Miscellaneous

10 Minute BD Checklist:

❑ M ❑ T ❑ W ❑ TH ❑ F

This Week's Gratitudes:

Weekend Recharging

Community & Connection

Pleasure Reading

Creativity & Beauty

Decadence/Splurge

Wellness & Movement

Appointments & Tasks

Companion Care/Other

Custom Category: _____

30 Minutes of Personal Development 2x Week:
☐ ☐

Why I Am Fabulous:

This Week's Goals:

WEEK OF _____

Highest Priority Work Activities

Long-term Projects To Keep An Eye On

Career/Business/Personal Development

Connecting/Networking

Miscellaneous

10 Minute BD Checklist:

❏ M ❏ T ❏ W ❏ TH ❏ F

This Week's Gratitudes:

Weekend Recharging

Pleasure Reading

Decadence/Splurge

Appointments & Tasks

Companion Care/Other

Custom Category: _____

30 Minutes of Personal Development 2x Week:
☐ ☐

Community & Connection

Creativity & Beauty

Wellness & Movement

Why I Am Fabulous:

> Summer summer summertime
> Time to sit back and unwind
> And think of the summers of the past
> Adjust the base and let the alpine blast
> Pop in my CD and let me run a rhyme
> And put your car on cruise and lay back
> 'Cause this is summertime
> – DJ Jazzy Jeff and Will Smith

Tie a Bow Around July

Things I Did Well

Challenges I Encountered

What I Am Grateful For This Month

AUGUST:
REST

In August, much of Paris is "ferme" – closed. While not a national holiday, it is a French cultural way of life that embraces the energy – and heat – of the year. August, along with January, are the lowest-energy months of the year. If your current calendar permits it, now is a good time for you to very intentionally slow yourself down, and embrace your inner French girl.

Maybe you can consider taking a couple of "summer Fridays" off? Make a batch of exotic popsicles filled with fresh berries. Peruse a farmer's market and buy a couple of fruits you've never tried before. Grill up some peaches and watermelon and bring them to a late-afternoon supper in the shade. Host a breakfast potluck picnic where the kids can run around while you sip iced coffee. Scent your pillowcases with lavender aromatherapy oil. Take long naps.

Slowing down will permit you to recharge your batteries for the upcoming autumn, so give yourself permission to really rest.

Inner Goal

Outer Goal

Professional Goal

LEARN TO RELAX. YOUR BODY IS PRECIOUS, AS IT HOUSES YOUR MIND AND SPIRIT. INNER PEACE BEGINS WITH A RELAXED BODY.
—NORMAN VINCENT PEALE

Month at a Glance

SUNDAY	MONDAY	TUESDAY	WEDNESDAY	THURSDAY	FRIDAY	SATURDAY

This Week's Goals:

WEEK OF _____

Highest Priority Work Activities

Long-term Projects To Keep An Eye On

Career/Business/Personal Development

Connecting/Networking

Miscellaneous

10 Minute BD Checklist:

❑ M ❑ T ❑ W ❑ TH ❑ F

This Week's Gratitudes:

Weekend Recharging

Pleasure Reading

Decadence/Splurge

Appointments & Tasks

Companion Care/Other

Custom Category: _____

30 Minutes of Personal Development 2x Week:
☐ ☐

Community & Connection

Creativity & Beauty

Wellness & Movement

Why I Am Fabulous:

This Week's Goals:

WEEK OF _____

Highest Priority Work Activities

Long-term Projects To Keep An Eye On

Career/Business/Personal Development

Connecting/Networking

Miscellaneous

10 Minute BD Checklist:

❏ M ❏ T ❏ W ❏ TH ❏ F

This Week's Gratitudes:

Weekend Recharging

Community & Connection

Pleasure Reading

Creativity & Beauty

Decadence/Splurge

Wellness & Movement

Appointments & Tasks

Companion Care/Other

Why I Am Fabulous:

Custom Category: _____

30 Minutes of Personal Development 2x Week:
☐ ☐

This Week's Goals:

WEEK OF _____

Highest Priority Work Activities

Long-term Projects To Keep An Eye On

Career/Business/Personal Development

Connecting/Networking

Miscellaneous

10 Minute BD Checklist:

☐ M ☐ T ☐ W ☐ TH ☐ F

This Week's Gratitudes:

Weekend Recharging

Community & Connection

Pleasure Reading

Creativity & Beauty

Decadence/Splurge

Wellness & Movement

Appointments & Tasks

Companion Care/Other

Custom Category: _____

30 Minutes of Personal Development 2x Week:
☐ ☐

Why I Am Fabulous:

This Week's Goals:

WEEK OF _____

Highest Priority Work Activities

Long-term Projects To Keep An Eye On

Career/Business/Personal Development

Connecting/Networking

Miscellaneous

10 Minute BD Checklist:

☐ M ☐ T ☐ W ☐ TH ☐ F

This Week's Gratitudes:

Weekend Recharging

Pleasure Reading

Decadence/Splurge

Appointments & Tasks

Companion Care/Other

Custom Category: _____

30 Minutes of Personal Development 2x Week:
☐ ☐

Community & Connection

Creativity & Beauty

Wellness & Movement

Why I Am Fabulous:

125

CREATE SPACE IN YOUR LIFE FOR BEAUTY.
— REGENA THOMASHAUER, AKA "MAMA GENA"

Tie a Bow Around August

Things I Did Well

Challenges I Encountered

What I Am Grateful For This Month

September: Back to School

It's time to start anew with the energy that comes from the "back to school" vibe. What personal and professional matters that may have fallen off the radar while you were taking your well-deserved summer siestas? Review the goals you set the last few months and check in with what worked and what needs your attention.

Additionally, have fun thinking about your professional persona and executive presence moving into the autumn, when all the new fall fashions are in the shops. Are there items you want to add to your wardrobe that can bring you more confidence and authority? Even if it's a red lipstick, sometimes the smallest props can make a difference.

Plan a celebration as well to wrap up Q3 and the gains you've made since June. Is there a new hotspot you'd like to try – or perhaps just cozy up with something decadent in front of a candlelit table in your home.

Inner Goal

Outer Goal

Professional Goal

Life starts all over again when it gets crisp in the fall.
F. Scott Fitzgerald, "The Great Gatsby"

Month at a Glance

SUNDAY	MONDAY	TUESDAY	WEDNESDAY	THURSDAY	FRIDAY	SATURDAY

This Week's Goals:

WEEK OF _____

Highest Priority Work Activities

Long-term Projects To Keep An Eye On

Career/Business/Personal Development

Connecting/Networking

Miscellaneous

10 Minute BD Checklist:

❏ M ❏ T ❏ W ❏ TH ❏ F

This Week's Gratitudes:

Weekend Recharging

Pleasure Reading

Decadence/Splurge

Appointments & Tasks

Companion Care/Other

Custom Category: _____

30 Minutes of Personal Development 2x Week:
❏ ❏

Community & Connection

Creativity & Beauty

Wellness & Movement

Why I Am Fabulous:

This Week's Goals:

WEEK OF _____

Highest Priority Work Activities

Long-term Projects To Keep An Eye On

Career/Business/Personal Development

Connecting/Networking

Miscellaneous

10 Minute BD Checklist:

❏ M ❏ T ❏ W ❏ TH ❏ F

This Week's Gratitudes:

Weekend Recharging

Pleasure Reading

Decadence/Splurge

Appointments & Tasks

Companion Care/Other

Custom Category: _____

30 Minutes of Personal Development 2x Week:
☐ ☐

Community & Connection

Creativity & Beauty

Wellness & Movement

Why I Am Fabulous:

This Week's Goals:

WEEK OF _____

Highest Priority Work Activities

Long-term Projects To Keep An Eye On

Career/Business/Personal Development

Connecting/Networking

Miscellaneous

10 Minute BD Checklist:

☐ M ☐ T ☐ W ☐ TH ☐ F

This Week's Gratitudes:

Weekend Recharging

Community & Connection

Pleasure Reading

Creativity & Beauty

Decadence/Splurge

Wellness & Movement

Appointments & Tasks

Companion Care/Other

Why I Am Fabulous:

Custom Category: _____

30 Minutes of Personal Development 2x Week:
❑ ❑

This Week's Goals:

WEEK OF _____

Highest Priority Work Activities

Long-term Projects To Keep An Eye On

Career/Business/Personal Development

Connecting/Networking

Miscellaneous

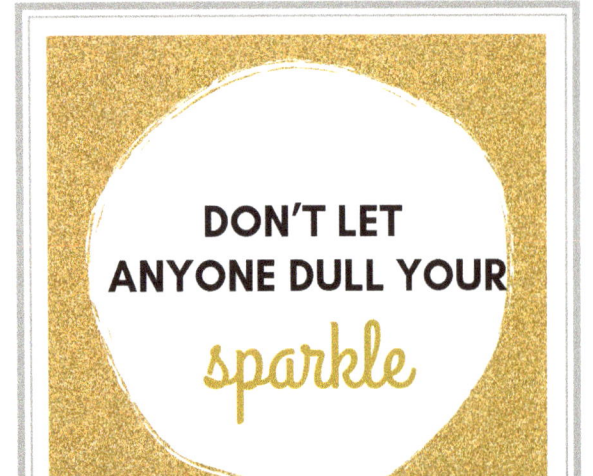

10 Minute BD Checklist:

❏ M ❏ T ❏ W ❏ TH ❏ F

This Week's Gratitudes:

Weekend Recharging

Pleasure Reading

Decadence/Splurge

Appointments & Tasks

Companion Care/Other

Custom Category: _____

30 Minutes of Personal Development 2x Week:
☐ ☐

Community & Connection

Creativity & Beauty

Wellness & Movement

Why I Am Fabulous:

> RENEWAL REQUIRES OPENING YOURSELF UP
> TO NEW WAYS OF THINKING AND FEELING.
> — DEBORAH DAY

Tie a Bow Around September

Things I Did Well

Challenges I Encountered

What I Am Grateful For This Month

Notes

> People rarely succeed unless they have fun in what they are doing.
> — Dale Carnegie

4TH QUARTER
AUTUMN

4TH QUARTER
HARVEST AND CELEBRATE

Congratulations! You are heading into the last quarter of the year. The days are getting longer and cooler, and the holiday season is soon upon us. Use this festive and celebratory energy to your benefit – how can you expand your professional reach and circles by harnessing the energy of this season? Our "Professional Success Strategies" section has ideas to help you end your year strong – and with a smile. Use this planner to prepare for any year-end reviews and self-assessments you may have. It's all here in front of you!

Here is your last official Wheel of Life for this year as well. How are your current numbers? How do you feel about them? Is there one particular area you might want to pay special VIP attention to, between now and the end of the year?

You are incredible and amazing. Own what a rock star you are, right here, right now:

I AM A ROCK STAR BECAUSE:

1.

2.

3.

Being a rockstar is the intersection of who you are and who you want to be.
— SLASH

Q4 Wheel of Life

This quarterly Wheel of Life is designed to have you honestly assess where you are, and where you need support, in each area.

ASSESSMENT:
On a scale of 0 (low) to 10 (high), where do you feel you are in each area? Mark that score on the Wheel.

REFLECTION:
What areas do you feel most need more attention, focus, resources, and support?

DESIGN:
For each area you feel needs more attention, design three action steps you will take to support this goal. What supports can you add? What pieces of your life can you simplify to focus attention on areas that want it?

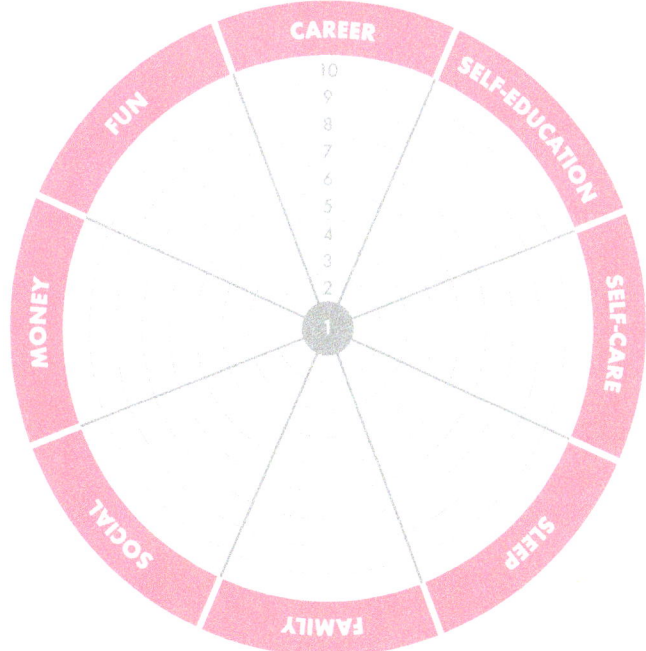

AREA: _____

Action Steps:

1.

2.

3.

AREA: _____

Action Steps:

1.

2.

3.

AREA: _____

Action Steps:

1.

2.

3.

Q4 CAREER DEVELOPMENT STRATEGIES

- ❏ Review all lists above. Review Q1, Q2, and Q3 plans – did you hit your goals? Try to complete any pieces you didn't do, and, as necessary, focus on completing your MAIN goals you had for your year (you can revisit the others next year!).

- ❏ Pull all information and data to send holiday cards with personalized notes to your clients, referral networks, and others you want to stay in contact with. Thank them for their business. Think as well about sending a "Happy New Year" card in lieu of a holiday card which you can send in January.

YOUR IDEAS:

- ❏ Review this planner and start strategizing your year-end review process. Where were you successful? What might you do differently?

- ❏ Plan something FABULOUS to celebrate YOU!

- ❏ Start thinking about your goals for next year and begin writing them down in this planner – or in a new journal. Think even bigger than you did this year!

- ❏ Complete organizing and executing your pro bono or nonprofit event that you may have started in Q3 (or begin now!). Enjoy the process of giving back to others as you build community and connections within your firm, company, or organization. Be sure you publicize this event and your leadership in it internally as well as externally, on social media as well as with media sources.

- ❏ Schedule a Halloween or holiday-themed happy hour for clients/referral sources/non-lawyer colleagues at your office or off-site.

- ❏ Send personal gifts to VIP clients and personal connections with a note of gratitude.

- ❏ Go onsite with a client or invite outside counsel to your office to review work, meet management and employees, see facilities, socialize, and discuss additional concerns.

- ❏ Attend at least one trade organization, bar association, or networking meeting per month.

Q4 Professional Goals

Q4 Personal Goals

Life is a party — dress for it.
— Audrey Hepburn

October: Mix and Mingle

The three-month season of frivolity and celebration is now upon us! The silly spookiness of Halloween leads to Thanksgiving, and then Hanukah, Christmas, and Kwanzaa . . . and before we know it, we'll be ringing in the New Year.

You might be in the mood for partying – or perhaps it's the last thing you feel like doing. Whatever your social predilection, think about moving yourself out of your customary comfort zones. If you like to work hard and party hard, perhaps take some contemplative alone time. If you prefer being a homebody, grab a wingperson and drop by a couple of soirees (see "Success as a Team Sport" ideas in the Professional Toolbox). This is a very good time to try building new networking muscles, which can build more career success.

No matter your style, inject some well-earned frivolity into your routine and see what shakes loose.

Inner Goal

Outer Goal

Professional Goal

> DRAMA IS VERY IMPORTANT IN LIFE: YOU HAVE TO COME ON WITH A BANG. YOU NEVER WANT TO GO OUT WITH A WHIMPER. EVERYTHING CAN HAVE DRAMA IF IT'S DONE RIGHT. EVEN A PANCAKE.
> JULIA CHILD

Month at a Glance

SUNDAY	MONDAY	TUESDAY	WEDNESDAY	THURSDAY	FRIDAY	SATURDAY

This Week's Goals:

WEEK OF _____

Highest Priority Work Activities

Long-term Projects To Keep An Eye On

Career/Business/Personal Development

Connecting/Networking

Miscellaneous

10 Minute BD Checklist:

❏ M ❏ T ❏ W ❏ TH ❏ F

This Week's Gratitudes:

Weekend Recharging

Pleasure Reading

Decadence/Splurge

Appointments & Tasks

Companion Care/Other

Custom Category: _____

30 Minutes of Personal Development 2x Week:
☐ ☐

Community & Connection

Creativity & Beauty

Wellness & Movement

Why I Am Fabulous:

This Week's Goals:

WEEK OF _____

Highest Priority Work Activities

Long-term Projects To Keep An Eye On

Career/Business/Personal Development

Connecting/Networking

Miscellaneous

10 Minute BD Checklist:

❏ M ❏ T ❏ W ❏ TH ❏ F

This Week's Gratitudes:

Weekend Recharging

Pleasure Reading

Decadence/Splurge

Appointments & Tasks

Companion Care/Other

Custom Category: _____

30 Minutes of Personal Development 2x Week:
☐ ☐

Community & Connection

Creativity & Beauty

Wellness & Movement

Why I Am Fabulous:

This Week's Goals:

WEEK OF _____

Highest Priority Work Activities

Long-term Projects To Keep An Eye On

Career/Business/Personal Development

Connecting/Networking

Miscellaneous

10 Minute BD Checklist:

☐ M ☐ T ☐ W ☐ TH ☐ F

This Week's Gratitudes:

Weekend Recharging

Pleasure Reading

Decadence/Splurge

Appointments & Tasks

Companion Care/Other

Custom Category: _____

30 Minutes of Personal Development 2x Week:
☐ ☐

Community & Connection

Creativity & Beauty

Wellness & Movement

Why I Am Fabulous:

This Week's Goals:

WEEK OF _____

Highest Priority Work Activities

Long-term Projects To Keep An Eye On

Career/Business/Personal Development

Connecting/Networking

Miscellaneous

10 Minute BD Checklist:

❏ M ❏ T ❏ W ❏ TH ❏ F

This Week's Gratitudes:

Weekend Recharging

Community & Connection

Pleasure Reading

Creativity & Beauty

Decadence/Splurge

Wellness & Movement

Appointments & Tasks

Companion Care/Other

Why I Am Fabulous:

Custom Category: _____

30 Minutes of Personal Development 2x Week:
☐ ☐

NOTES

There is more to life than increasing its speed.
— MAHATMA GANDHI

Tie a Bow Around October

Things I Did Well

Challenges I Encountered

What I Am Grateful For This Month

NOVEMBER: STRESS LESS

With the mania of the holidays (aka the "holi-daze") upon us, consider making a more intentional effort to take extra-special care of yourself to combat some of the inevitable holiday and end-of-year work stress. Whether it's FOMO, end of year reviews, family drama, or financial pressure, having easy-to-access well-being tools can help you balance this time of year. This planner is full of ideas — look through the toolboxes and mark off what you can add to your routine.

Another way to cut some of the stress and pressure is not only to be grateful for what you have, but to intentionally be extra-generous to those who have much less. Sometimes the more you give to others, the more peace of mind you actually get in return.

And consider saying "no" to anything you don't have to do at this time of year. The more you say "no" to the unnecessary, the more you are actually saying "yes" to you.

Inner Goal

Outer Goal

Professional Goal

MAY YOUR WALLS KNOW JOY, MAY EVERY ROOM HOLD LAUGHTER,
AND EVERY WINDOW BE OPEN TO GREAT POSSIBILITY.
MARY ANN RADMACHER

Month at a Glance

SUNDAY	MONDAY	TUESDAY	WEDNESDAY	THURSDAY	FRIDAY	SATURDAY

This Week's Goals:

WEEK OF _____

Highest Priority Work Activities

Long-term Projects To Keep An Eye On

Career/Business/Personal Development

Connecting/Networking

Miscellaneous

COZY = HAPPY

10 Minute BD Checklist:

☐ M ☐ T ☐ W ☐ TH ☐ F

This Week's Gratitudes:

Weekend Recharging

Pleasure Reading

Decadence/Splurge

Appointments & Tasks

Companion Care/Other

Custom Category: _____

30 Minutes of Personal Development 2x Week:
☐ ☐

Community & Connection

Creativity & Beauty

Wellness & Movement

Why I Am Fabulous:

This Week's Goals:

WEEK OF _____

Highest Priority Work Activities

Long-term Projects To Keep An Eye On

Career/Business/Personal Development

Connecting/Networking

Miscellaneous

10 Minute BD Checklist:

❏ M ❏ T ❏ W ❏ TH ❏ F

This Week's Gratitudes:

Weekend Recharging

Community & Connection

Pleasure Reading

Creativity & Beauty

Decadence/Splurge

Wellness & Movement

Appointments & Tasks

Companion Care/Other

Why I Am Fabulous:

Custom Category: _____

30 Minutes of Personal Development 2x Week:
☐ ☐

This Week's Goals:

WEEK OF _____

Highest Priority Work Activities

Long-term Projects To Keep An Eye On

Career/Business/Personal Development

Connecting/Networking

Miscellaneous

10 Minute BD Checklist:

❏ M ❏ T ❏ W ❏ TH ❏ F

This Week's Gratitudes:

Weekend Recharging

Pleasure Reading

Decadence/Splurge

Appointments & Tasks

Companion Care/Other

Custom Category: _____

30 Minutes of Personal Development 2x Week:
☐ ☐

Community & Connection

Creativity & Beauty

Wellness & Movement

Why I am Fabulous:

165

This Week's Goals:

WEEK OF _____

Highest Priority Work Activities

Long-term Projects To Keep An Eye On

Career/Business/Personal Development

Connecting/Networking

Miscellaneous

10 Minute BD Checklist:

☐ M ☐ T ☐ W ☐ TH ☐ F

This Week's Gratitudes:

Weekend Recharging

Community & Connection

Pleasure Reading

Creativity & Beauty

Decadence/Splurge

Wellness & Movement

Appointments & Tasks

Companion Care/Other

Custom Category: _____

30 Minutes of Personal Development 2x Week:
☐ ☐

Why I Am Fabulous:

I THINK I'LL WORK ALL MY LIFE.
WHEN YOU'RE HAVING FUN, WHY STOP HAVING FUN?
— HELEN THOMAS

Tie a Bow Around November

Things I Did Well

Challenges I Encountered

What I Am Grateful For This Month

NOTES

Learn to be thankful for what you already have, while you pursue all that you want.

— JIM ROHN

CELEBRATE!
HOLIDAY

December: Celebrate!

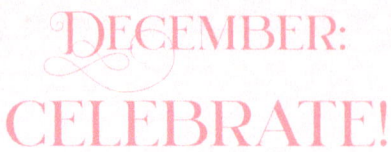

Pop the bubbly and begin the process of wrapping a bow around your year. Yes, there is a lot to do and yes, you will get it done. Postpone anything non-essential until next year, and focus on the *now*. Take a few moments to review this journal as you prepare for any year-end reviews, as it contains wonderful details of your year. Reflect on how you've grown this year – how you pushed yourself, celebrated yourself, adorned yourself, challenged yourself. Even if you didn't do as much as you intended, that doesn't matter! The most important thing is that you dreamed, you acted, your contemplated, you were generous, appreciative, and full of gratitude. You acknowledged how fabulous you are. You. Are. Amazing!!

Appreciate all the opportunities and challenges you've been given. Be generous to those around you, particularly those less fortunate than you. Remember, the more you give, the more you get.

Congratulations on an Amazing Year!

Inner Goal

Outer Goal

Professional Goal

Life is short. Wear your party pants.
— Loretta LaRoche

Month at a Glance

SUNDAY	MONDAY	TUESDAY	WEDNESDAY	THURSDAY	FRIDAY	SATURDAY

This Week's Goals:

WEEK OF _____

Highest Priority Work Activities

Long-term Projects To Keep An Eye On

Career/Business/Personal Development

Connecting/Networking

Miscellaneous

CULTIVATE A LITTLE MYSTERY

10 Minute BD Checklist:

❏ M ❏ T ❏ W ❏ TH ❏ F

This Week's Gratitudes:

Weekend Recharging

Community & Connection

Pleasure Reading

Creativity & Beauty

Decadence/Splurge

Wellness & Movement

Appointments & Tasks

Companion Care/Other

Custom Category: _____

30 Minutes of Personal Development 2x Week:
☐ ☐

Why I Am Fabulous:

This Week's Goals:

WEEK OF _____

Highest Priority Work Activities

Long-term Projects To Keep An Eye On

Career/Business/Personal Development

Connecting/Networking

Miscellaneous

10 Minute BD Checklist:

☐ M ☐ T ☐ W ☐ TH ☐ F

This Week's Gratitudes:

Weekend Recharging

Pleasure Reading

Decadence/Splurge

Appointments & Tasks

Companion Care/Other

Custom Category: _____

30 Minutes of Personal Development 2x Week:
❏ ❏

Community & Connection

Creativity & Beauty

Wellness & Movement

Why I am Fabulous:

This Week's Goals:

WEEK OF _____

Highest Priority Work Activities

Long-term Projects To Keep An Eye On

Career/Business/Personal Development

Connecting/Networking

Miscellaneous

10 Minute BD Checklist:

❏ M ❏ T ❏ W ❏ TH ❏ F

This Week's Gratitudes:

Weekend Recharging

Pleasure Reading

Decadence/Splurge

Appointments & Tasks

Companion Care/Other

Custom Category: _____

30 Minutes of Personal Development 2x Week:
☐ ☐

Community & Connection

Creativity & Beauty

Wellness & Movement

Why I Am Fabulous:

This Week's Goals:

WEEK OF _____

Highest Priority Work Activities

Long-term Projects To Keep An Eye On

Career/Business/Personal Development

Connecting/Networking

Miscellaneous

10 Minute BD Checklist:

❏ M ❏ T ❏ W ❏ TH ❏ F

This Week's Gratitudes:

Weekend Recharging

Pleasure Reading

Decadence/Splurge

Appointments & Tasks

Companion Care/Other

Custom Category: _____

30 Minutes of Personal Development 2x Week:
❏ ❏

Community & Connection

Creativity & Beauty

Wellness & Movement

Why I Am Fabulous:

Commit to being an overachiever in the fun department.
— Regena Thomashauer, aka Mama Gena

Tie a Bow Around December

Things I Did Well

Challenges I Encountered

What I Am Grateful For This Month

> Some 80% of your life is spent working. You want to have fun at home; why shouldn't you have fun at work?
> – Richard Branson

Personal Toolbox

Recommended Reading for Instant Elevation

Below is a selection of books that never fail to give me a dose of instant inspiration and energy (I do love instant gratification!). Even just 5-10 minutes with one of these friends leaves me feeling elevated. I hope you find some inspiration in their pages, too.

Start Right Where You Are by Sam Bennett

GuRU by RuPaul Charles

My Life in France by Julia Child

The Seven Spiritual Laws of Success by Deepak Chopra

Eccentric Glamour by Simon Doonan

A Year of Style by Frederic Fekkai

New and Select Poems by Mary Oliver

Entre Nous: A Woman's Guide to Finding Her Inner French Girl by Debra Olliver

Living Juicy – Daily Morsels for Your Creative Soul by SARK (aka Susan Kennedy)

Succulent Wild Woman by SARK (aka Susan Kennedy)

La Seduction (How the French Play the Game of Life) by Elaine Sciolino

A Book That Takes Its Time: An Unhurried Adventure in Creative Mindfulness by Irene Smit and Astrid van der Hulst (a Flow book)

Empress of Fashion: A Life of Diana Vreeland by Amanda Mackenzie Stuart

Mama Gena's School of Womanly Arts by Regena Thomashauer

DV by Diana Vreeland

Your Beauty Mark by Dita von Teese

The Diva Rules by Michelle Visage

Tranquilologie: A DIY Guide to Everyday Tranquility by Kimberly Wilson

Tranquility du Jour by Kimberly Wilson

 Check out Kimberly Wilson's **Tranqility du Jour podcast/app** for addition inspiration.

Creativity and Beauty

- Buy flowers for your office on a regular basis.

- Buy a book, take a course in, or check out videos on hand lettering and start writing with a flourish.

- Put some beautiful inspiring art in your office.

- Learn new ways to wrap a scarf.

- Paint your nails an adventurous new color.

- Become a photojournalist: take pictures each week on a new theme (flowers, holiday decorations, dogs, bakery and bookstore windows, etc.).

- Read or write a new poem every day (download a poetry app to make it easy!).

- Linger in a bookshop or museum.

- Eat a new food every day, or try some new spices in your cooking.

- Bake something ridiculously decadent and crazy!

- Plant an herb garden.

- Make a Green Goddess Smoothie and build beauty from the inside out.

- Go to a department store and smell some new perfumes.

- Take a few extra minutes every day to adorn yourself.

- Wear sequins to the office.

- Use a pink umbrella in the rain.

- Watch old movies! (Think Marilyn Monroe, Dorothy Dandridge, Gene Kelly, Fred Astaire, Audrey Hepburn, Alfred Hitchcock, etc.).

Your Ideas:

Community and Connection

- Make a date with a best friend who you don't see enough.
- Call up friends to tell them how much you love them and what makes them special to you.
- Plan a special party to celebrate a best friend's birthday.
- Sign up for a 5k and raise funds for a nonprofit whose cause is important to you.
- Volunteer to host your next family holiday dinner.
- Check out a new local organization or nonprofit.
- Find a therapist to help you feel less "stuck" if you feel like something is standing in the way of your connecting with others.
- Organize a girls' trip.
- Attend a rally to support or protest a cause important to you.
- Volunteer to help with an office community project or suggest one of your own.
- Keep money/items of need in your handbag to give to homeless people (a ziplock with $5, a couple of hand-warming packets, some handwipes, and a couple of granola bars).
- Offer to babysit so a friend can have a night out.
- Do acts of anonymous good (leave flowers for a coworker you know is going through a hard time, buy coffee for the person behind you in line, etc.).
- Get involved in a new church committee, or check out churches if you've been meaning to find one.
- Write two love notes per week to friends; keep some beautiful stationery and stamps at your desk to make it easy.
- Volunteer to mentor someone.
- Organize a bake sale for your kids' school.
- Give compliments to strangers.
- Give kudos or write a nice review to a colleague on LinkedIn.
- Try out a new class (hand lettering, dancing, massage, presentation skills, coding, etc.).
- Sign up for a retreat with a women's group you find interesting.
- Go on an early-morning hike with friends.
- Organize a block party.
- Vote! Help others register to vote.
- Bake some cookies and send them to family members with a love note.

Decadence/Splurge

- Buy a fabulous bottle of champagne and share it with friends "just because."

- Go to dinner and order dessert first.

- Order what you *really* want on the menu.

- Research an amazing vacation (even if you don't have the budget to actually go on one)!

- Bake something decadent . . . then add extra sprinkles!

- Buy super-soft organic sheets.

- Dress like today is a party!

- Use your "good" china at work, and at home.

- Make an extra-generous donation to a local animal shelter or other nonprofit you really care about.

- Add extra sparkle to your mani-pedis.

- Wear red lipstick to do something mundane.

- Visit a local farmer's market and pretend you are the South of France.

- Take yourself to high tea at a local tea shop or hotel.

- Try a fancy new hairstyle (braids, an updo, etc.).

- Invest in a new matching set of lingerie.

- Spray perfume in your lingerie and sock drawers.

- Get your car detailed.

- Take a tango/ballet/belly dancing class.

- Use extravagant gestures!

- Wear an armful of bangles – more is more!

- Send your mom/mentor/bestie some flowers; I'm also partial to the beautiful ones that last for a year by Venus et Fleur, which my bestie sent ME!

- Practice a new language on a free language app.

- Practice some extravagant hand-lettering.

- Use glittery body powder every day!

Your Ideas:

Weekend Recharging

- ❑ Explore a local farmer's market. Buy something quintessentially in season and try something new. Buy some flowers you can place throughout your home (including one on your bedstand!).

- ❑ Wake up extra early and take an invigorating extra-long walk! Use this time to make calls, or listen to podcasts or books on tape. Challenge your body and your mind.

- ❑ Make a list of things you are procrastinating about – and knock one thing off your list every weekend! Notice how this makes you feel and how it frees up mental energy, too.

- ❑ Peruse a local bookseller and buy a book of poetry.

- ❑ Journal! Document why you were fabulous this day, week, month. Or continue polishing your goal list.

- ❑ Plan an adventure: grab a girlfriend and go on a hike, or visit an amusement park.

- ❑ Take a nap.

- ❑ Buy a ticket for a local theater production – take yourself to dinner first (or after), and dress up!

- ❑ Plan a potluck and have friends bring over their favorite dishes.

- ❑ Take a yoga class (or watch one online).

- ❑ Write a letter to tell someone you love them.

- ❑ Make some Green Goddess Smoothie. Enjoy it all weekend.

- ❑ Research your exotic next vacation.

Sunday Self-Care:

As the end of the weekend comes to a close, anxiety levels can increase; some call it the "Sunday Scaries." I, however, prefer to remind myself to make the time to take extra-beautiful care of myself so I'm ready for the exciting week ahead. Ideas:

- Take a bath or beautiful hot shower and use your favorite body lotion after.
- Place fresh linens on your bed and spray them with an aromatherapy spray.
- Write out your professional and personal goals for the week in this planner.
- Journal about your weekend, goals, and dreams.
- Organize your bag and briefcase for the week ahead.
- Make a beautiful hot cup of your favorite non-caffeinated tea.
- Watch a dreamy old Hollywood movie (nothing scary and nothing violent!).
- Go to bed early.

Wellness and Movement

- Keep and smell some mint and citrus essential oils at your desk to enjoy during the day.
- Make regular donations to charitable causes you support.
- Be a flaneur; walk and observe the world around you.
- Drink at least 6 glasses of water a day. Yes, coffee counts; so does soup, smoothies, etc.
- Make a "Kickass Wellness" super-fun high-energy playlist.
- Try a new exercise class (barre, spinning, belly dancing, etc.).
- Spend some time in a flotation or isolation tank.
- Take an office dance break!
- Leave an anonymous gift for a coworker who you know is going through a hard time.
- Create a bath/shower ritual for yourself; use beautiful soaps, bath/shower fizzes, and special lotions.
- Go to bed 30 minutes early.
- Stretch every hour! Download a "desk yoga" app for ideas. Neck and shoulder rolls for starters can make a world of difference.
- Invest in a beautiful set of organic sheets.
- Keep flowers at your desk.
- Spend 5 minutes in nature every day (even if that means just visiting a flower stand).
- Keep some beautiful hand lotion at your desk.
- Use sunscreen!
- Keep a delicious array of herbal teas at your desk; drink your tea from a china cup.
- Cut back on dairy; try some vegan cheese options, and notice a difference in your skin.
- Try a Pilates reformer class (enjoy the springs and bounciness!).
- Journal "Why I Am Fabulous" at night before falling asleep.
- Take a walk around the block each afternoon to revive your energy.
- Try dry skin brushing before bathing.
- Drink the Green Goddess Smoothie.
- Experiment with a "digital detox" (try starting with just one hour).
- Recharge your phone at night somewhere other than next to your bed.
- Give yourself head massages (maybe buy an inexpensive scalp massager and keep it at your desk).

Glowing Goddess Smoothie

In order to be balanced, one must choose foods that inspire energy and glow. Below is a smoothie I've been drinking for several years that is adapted from the "Glowing Green Smoothie" from the book *The Beauty Detox Foods* by Kimberly Snyder, C.N. The amount of nutrients and energy in this drink is totally ridiculous and amazing!

Don't be afraid of the super-vibrant green color – the veggie flavors are more than balanced out by the fruit – and you can customize the recipe as you see fit. As your taste buds adapt to liquid greenery, you can play with the recipe to include more veggies as you wish. And use as many organic ingredients as you can, particularly because when using the skins (like for the apple and pear), you obviously want as few chemicals as possible in your healthy creation.

One benefit of this smoothie is that it will last you 3-4 days – so pop it in the fridge (I just leave it in my Vitamix blender with the cap on) and then just re-blend it for a few seconds to have a fresh cup every day for the better part of a week!

The best tool to make this is a Vitamix. Start with the veggies which need more time to pulverize; then add the fruit until it's all whipped and frothy.

INGREDIENTS:

- 2 cups filtered cold water
- 7 cups baby spinach (one bag's worth at the supermarket)
- 1 big head of romaine lettuce (if romaine is not available, just double up on the spinach)
- 2 stalks celery
- 1 cucumber (peeled if it isn't organic)
- 1 apple, cored and chopped (I like Fuji ones myself – they are sweeter)
- 1 pear, cored and chopped
- 1 banana
- Juice of 1 lemon (just squeeze it in)
- Piece of ginger (to your taste)
- Fresh or frozen berries of choice – I particularly love strawberries, blueberries, and pineapple. In the summer I tend to throw in whatever is in season!

DIRECTIONS:

Add water and a couple of fistfuls of spinach or romaine to the Vitamix. Starting the blender on low speed – then increasing to maximum velocity – mix until smooth. This creates a good base so the Vitamix can mix the rest of the ingredients without getting jammed with too many veggies. Repeat until all the greens have been blended, then add fruit and ginger.

Rosé All Day?

Being an attorney is totally hard, and add that to LIFE (social pressures, dating, being a mom, home responsibilities, etc.). Therefore, it is understandable to relax with a glass of wine or two at the end of a long day. However, many of us turn to alcohol or other substances as a crutch to cope with the pressure. Studies published by the ABA show that 1 in 5 practicing attorneys currently have a substance abuse disorder (twice the national average), and more are experiencing depression and anxiety. Add to this that the alcohol industry directs a lot of its energy towards encouraging women to drink ("mommy juice," "rosé all day" and all the girl-power "you deserve it" branding and fruit and candy flavorings). The result of all this, according to a JAMA Psychiatry study released in 2017, is the rate of alcohol abuse and dependence in women increased by 83.7 percent between 2002 and 2013.

If you are interested in exploring this issue, below please find some resources to help you understand what may be occurring and ways to find assistance for yourself or someone you care about (some call it the "sober curious" movement). This list is not remotely comprehensive, but is just a start to help you begin handling the stress and letting you know you are not alone.

- **Lawyer Assistance Programs (LAP) –** Check with your local bar association.

- **Talkspace –** An app to connect you with a therapist at your convenience

- *Girl Walks Out Of A Bar: A Memoir* by Lisa Smith (2016) Synopsis: Lisa Smith was a bright, young lawyer at a prestigious firm in NYC when alcoholism started to take over her life. What was once a way of escaping her insecurity and negativity became a means of coping with the anxiety and stress of an impossible workload. . . .

ONLINE COMMUNITIES AND PROGRAMS

Look online and on Instagram for instant assistance and inspiration . . . which will lead you to others. Here are some options:

- **The Temper:** TheTemper.com and @TheTemper

- LauraMcKowen.com and @Laura McKowen

- **Alcoholics Anonymous** and other organizations of that nature; look for meetings that may fit your schedule.

- **A Sober Girls Guide:** ASoberGirlsGuide.com and @ASoberGirlsGuide

If you are in an acute situation, and feel you may cause harm to yourself, reach out 24 hours per day to the National Suicide Prevention Lifeline (www.suicidepreventionlifeline.org), at 1-800-273-8255.

"YOU HAVE BRAINS IN YOUR HEAD. YOU HAVE FEET IN YOUR SHOES.
YOU CAN STEER YOURSELF ANY DIRECTION YOU CHOOSE.
YOU'RE ON YOUR OWN. AND YOU KNOW WHAT YOU KNOW.
AND YOU ARE THE ONE WHO'LL DECIDE WHERE TO GO."

– DR. SEUSS

Professional Toolbox

BD Action Steps – Just 10 Minutes a Day

Here is a list of quick ways you can spend only 10 minutes to build your business development muscles. Notice how doing something every day makes you feel.

- ❑ Research a current client's needs – research their organization, check out recent press, sign up for bulletins, review their SEC filings, sign up for Google alerts, etc. Use this information when reaching out to your contacts.

- ❑ For in-house, nonprofit, and government attorneys, cultivate friends, allies, and connections in departments outside your own. Building a personal brand in organizations that have many kinds of professionals requires you to develop communications and sales skills that are relatable to non-lawyers, and make connections up and down the org chart. Think about inviting people from operations, tax, development, R&D, etc. to coffee, lunch, events both inside and outside the org, and of course connect and support them on LinkedIn.

- ❑ Reach out to contacts you haven't reached out to in a while. Do you have time to schedule coffee or lunch? If nothing else, say hello.

- ❑ Send a recent client alert, article, blog post, or other piece to colleagues, current or former clients, and prospects – show that you are thinking of them and write a note reflecting how this alert may impact their businesses.

- ❑ Build your LinkedIn network – send invitations with a friendly personalized note to fellow alums, colleagues, and others. After you connect, send a note thanking them for joining your network and tell them to have a lovely day, weekend, or ask about something personal.

- ❑ Post content on LinkedIn – something you've written, a colleague authored, your firm or company posted, or something you find interesting – with an engaging note about its content. Spend some time on LinkedIn joining groups and contributing to those conversations.

- ❑ Read or listen to a career development or personal development book (see my recommended reading list if you need ideas).

- ❑ Research "hot topics" in your area of practice for an article, CLE presentation, or blog post series.

- ❑ Ask a more senior partner or colleague if you can help them with anything. Bring an idea or interesting piece of news to share as you have this facetime.

- Read your monthly ABA Journal or local bar association journal from beginning to end, and send complimentary emails to the authors of articles you most enjoyed.

- Send "it was lovely to meet you" emails to people you met the last week at networking, work, or social events.

- Research networking organizations in your area (not just legal organizations, but trade associations and the like) and put their next meeting on your agenda.

- Practice your "elevator pitch" – does it reflect the passion you have for your work? Is it fun to say? If it feels "too salesy," convoluted, or forced, write and practice a new one.

- Check out some cool new women's entrepreneurial organizations in your area to consider joining.

- Begin writing a blog post for your firm or organization's blog and work on it a little bit every day.

- Make a coffee date with a colleague in another practice area and talk about your practices.

- Make a list of people you know from school, socially, etc. in other industries – finance, accounting, healthcare, engineering, etc. Reach out to those people on LinkedIn.

- Look at your local bar association website and think about committees you may be interested in. Put their next meeting on your calendar.

- Talk to a business development coach at your law firm or company.

- Schedule "BD brainstorming" sessions with friends at your firm or company – think about ways you can work together to develop your careers and businesses.

- Register for CLE courses on attorney advertising and other BD-related areas.

- Make a list of colleagues/friends who you might be able to send business to. The more business *you* give to people, the more they will think about business to send to you.

- Practice your presentation skills – for starters, leave a couple of practice voicemails to yourself on (a) a serious professional topic; and (b) a social invitation. Does your voice – tenor and content – reflect who you are trying to project in each scenario? Are there ways to alter your presentation to more accurately present yourself?

- Polish up your bio on your firm or company website, and on LinkedIn add more representative matters, areas of practice, and other dynamic details and descriptions.

- Go online or window shopping for suits, other pieces of clothing, and even accessories that might upgrade your current wardrobe so you feel more confident and project more power.

- Organize your office and decide what you might want to add to upgrade its appearance. Remember, your office is a reflection of yourself.

- Check out interesting TED talks. I recommend starting with Amy Cuddy's "Your Body Language May Shape Who You Are" presentation.

Big Ticket Career Development

In addition to your daily career development steps, think about embarking upon some bigger projects that can have major payoffs for your career and will reflect your leadership in other ways. Some of these items will cost money from your own pocket – don't let that stop you (and check with your accountant what you might be able to write off your taxes). Invest in yourself without hesitation. This can include:

- Become an adjunct law professor at a local law school. Research and outline a class you can teach – or simply offer your ability to do a training or presentation. If it is local, start with your alma mater – it's an easier sell to go back to where your career started and they likely still remember you. If you don't feel you are an expert in a particular area, volunteer to teach a legal writing class or an entry-level skills course.

- Volunteer for leadership not only in local bar associations, but also in statewide and national associations – and go up the ladder.

- Research joining nonprofit and corporate Boards of Directors.

- Publish regularly through a variety of mediums – law review articles, legal thought pieces, blog posts, even LinkedIn pieces. Everyone needs content – research and offer pieces (or an article series!) to local, regional, or even national media channels.

- Join and become a leader in a local chamber of commerce or trade association. Become a leader to the community, not just in the legal industry.

- Invest in exceptional headshots, media trainings, and other courses that will polish your public persona. Invest in your own personal "glam squad" for events.

- Hire your own PR company to help promote any of the endeavors above, and to get your name out there.

- Write a book – it could be fiction, non-fiction, or something related to the law. It's a calling card that very few people have. Self-publishing is an easy way to do this if you can't get a publisher (and hire a designer to make it look professional).

- Think about becoming known for a certain holiday or themed party. Perhaps you host a kicking Halloween party, or put together really intimate networking events for women professionals in your industry. Have people look forward to your annual shindig!

- Dress for the job you want, not the one you have. Invest in quality and/or designer clothes that look top-notch and reflects your executive presence. Check out consignment sites like TheRealReal for authentic and well-kept pieces.

- Upgrade your office design so it looks like the office of a rainmaker, general counsel, or business leader. Consider: art, rugs, special accessories (Kate Spade has nice ones), and keep it tidy. Notice how being in your lovely office makes you feel.

- Hire an Executive Coach to help you develop your skill set and polish your executive presence as you head up the career ladder.

Success Is a Team Sport

One of my favorite sayings is: Success Is a Team Sport. No one becomes wealthy or wildly successful on their own (as Jim Rohn would say – "it's hard to find a rich hermit"). In addition to your individual career development initiatives, think about creating joint ventures with colleagues both inside and outside of your employment. Doing things together can make things more fun, less daunting, and can provide support in areas where you feel challenged (now you have a wingperson to take with you to a networking event, for example). You can get more bang for the buck in terms of advertising, cross-selling, budgeting, and workload distribution. Here are some ideas:

- Become a networking team. Divide pre-event research, and even "working" the event itself. Introduce each other with detailed and sincere compliments, which will reflect: (a) your graciousness; (b) makes talking about yourself much easier as someone else is actually doing it; and (c) shows people how wonderful it could be work with you both. Divide the follow-up from each networking event, copying the other on your "nice to meet you" emails and any additional conversations that come from them.

- Invite a colleague to help you put together a CLE program, with the two of you as presenters and pitch it together.

- Polish your elevator pitches, executive presence, and other skills on each other in a safe and supportive environment.

- Co-lead a company mentoring circle or training program.

- Co-sponsor and co-host social events for clients, prospects, and referral sources.

- Co-sponsor and co-host community and nonprofit events which can expose both of you to people in your communities while doing good for others.

- Share each other's LinkedIn postings to get twice the exposure.

- Co-author an article or blog post series.

- Share the expense of an event sponsorship.

- Share the expense of hiring a personal PR representative.

- Share donation credit for a generous contribution to a nonprofit initative.

Your Ideas:

Success Key: Personal Development

In your quest for excellence and balance, there is one last key that will unlock all sorts of magic: investing in your personal development. Personal development is about achieving your fullest potential. Makes sense – to be anything great, be it a parent, partner, artist, writer, baker, athlete, actress, business leader, or attorney – you have to study the craft of each. When you are planning your next deal or trial, you strategize and prepare for the variables of those occasions. The same needs to hold true for yourself and your personal life and goals.

As Jim Rohn put it: "Work hard on your job and you can make a living. Work hard on yourself and you can make a fortune."

Your "fortune" can be anything you want it to be – we all define wealth differently. What might that look like for you?

The following resources are great places to start – either in written form or via audiobooks (I'm a huge fan of listening to them during my daily commutes). They are considered classics for a reason. And they are fun to listen to!

- *7 Habits of Highly Effective People* by Stephen Covey
- *Secrets of the Millionaire Mind* by T. Harv Eker
- *Think and Grow Rich* by Napoleon Hill (I recommend the updated 21st century edition – and it contains quantum energy principles way ahead of its time.)
- *The Art of Exceptional Living* by Jim Rohn
- *Mama Gena's School of Womanly Arts* by Regena Thomashauer

In addition, find inspiration in reading the biographies or autobiographies of business leaders and creatives. Some ideas: Steve Jobs, Michelle Obama, Mary Kay Ash, Richard Branson, Diane von Furstenberg, and Diana Vreeland.

There is a checklist at the bottom of your weekly planner pages asking you to invest 30 minutes twice a week in your personal development. Start checking this off and notice how taking this time for yourself makes you feel.

Life is not about finding yourself. It is about creating yourself.
George Bernard Shaw

Career Development Reading Resources

Here is a curated list of books that contain amazing career development ideas and inspirational support. I know you want quick results, so schedule just 5 minutes a day flipping through any of these books and see what jumps out at you (keep it on your desk so you don't forget to dedicate this time for yourself). If, due to your particular area of practice, some advice does not appear directly applicable to you, see what pieces you can apply to yourself and your developing skill set. Identify just one area that would be fun to try and add it to your planner list. Maybe ask a favorite colleague to read one along with you and design some joint career development plans. Make your success a team sport! And, very importantly, notice how learning new things makes you feel. Brava for all your efforts!

CAREER DEVELOPMENT RESOURCES:

Fishman, Ross:
The Ultimate Law Firm Associate's Marketing Checklist

Hedges, Kristi:
The Power of Presence

Haserot, Phyllis:
The Marketer's Handbook of Tips and Checklists

Maraia, Mark M.:
Rainmaking Made Simple

Snyder, Theda:
Women Rainmakers' 101+ Best Marketing Tips

Taheripour, Mori:
Bring Yourself: How to Harness the Power of Connection to Negotiate Fearlessly

Women Rainmakers' Best Marketing Tips
(ABA Law Practice Management Section publication)

FOR QUICK FOCUS & INSPIRATION:

Arden, Paul:
Whatever You Think, Think the Opposite

It's Not How Good You Are, It's How Good You Want to Be

Bennett, Sam:
Start Right Where You Are (the audiobook is excellent too!)

Chopra, Deepak:
Seven Spiritual Laws of Success (love the audiobook as well)

Gitomer, Jeffrey:
Little Black Book of Connections
Little Black Book of Selling
Little Gold Book of YES! Attitude
Little Teal Book of Trust

Check out the **Blinkist app** for quick 15-minute summaries of a huge number of business and personal development books (subscription required).

Inner, Outer, and Professional Monthly Goals

Identifying your goals helps you sharpen where you think you can use additional focus and support. Each month's introduction and theme pages contain spaces for you to identify three kinds of goals:

- Inner (spiritual, psychological, emotional)
- Outer (physical, environmental, social)
- Professional (job, career development, professional development)

Think about these goals as you identify the actions you wish to take on your weekly planner pages. You can carry your goals from month to month, or switch them out depending on what is going on in your life. Here are some goals I've used if these give you some ideas:

INNER:
The most important project I will ever work on is myself.
Be better this month than you were last month.
Discipline = Freedom.
Amazing new doors open for me every day.

OUTER:
Dance! Every dance is an offering to god.
Slow down and soften. Breathe. Stretch.
Say YES more often.
Be photo-ready wherever you are.

PROFESSIONAL:
Power posing practice.
Office beautification project.
Executive presence polishing.
Keep writing. Cultivate thought leadership.

The first step is the hardest — making a commitment to yourself, for yourself.
— Mary Kay Ash

The French Macaron Theory

This theory suggests that jumping into the deep end and propelling yourself beyond your comfort zone can make things much easier than slowly easing your way into anything. I've loved macarons since I first ate my first one in Paris in 2004. When I decided to start baking in 2018 (after weeks of binge-watching Halloween and Christmas baking shows on the Food Network), I bought a yellow KitchenAid mixer and decided to make pink French macarons. Macarons (as explained in all the shows I watched) are one of the hardest things to successfully bake even for an expert, never mind someone with literally no experience like me.

I spent an afternoon coated in confectioner's sugar and my kitchen and dining room covered with equipment of all types (candy thermometer, infrared thermometer, measuring cups, piping bags, electronic scale, parchment paper, trays, sanding sugar, sifters, food coloring). During the very messy and occasionally frenetic activities, the macarons were whipped, piped, slammed (literally) on the counters to remove air bubbles, rested, baked at two temperatures, cooled, and then filled with lemon curd and Nutella. All that work for about 20 rather misshapen yet tasty macarons.

I now know I can bake anything. Nothing intimidates me or is too challenging. Since I started with the hardest thing to bake, everything (literally) is a cakewalk.

Think about how this can apply to other activities. If we do something really challenging and push our limits, we know we can do anything less strenuous. For example:

- One weekend, push yourself to walk (or run) 5 miles. Now you know you can do a 5k (3.1 miles) for sure.
- Write a white paper or detailed legal article on a hot topic you're interested in knowing more about. Now you know you can author blog posts with ease.
- Organize and deliver a one-hour CLE program (with the required attendant written materials). Now you know you can make a short presentation on the topic to a client or prospect.

Where can you push yourself just a bit more past your comfort zone?

Acknowledgements

This planner was inspired by, and is the culmination of, all the guidance and inspiration I experience each and every day from so many teachers, friends, family, clients, colleagues, and guides of many kinds.

I'd like to thank the three major teachers in my life:

- PHILIP J. HIRSCHKOP, who taught me to practice law with heart, a sense of humor (and even silliness), and the deepest integrity. Thank you for opening up the door to my family, and for making my professional dreams come true;
- FRANK R. PARKER, who taught me justice is a life-long endeavor and that life is all too fleeting; and
- REGENA THOMASHAUER, who taught me that pleasure is, in fact, an essential daily nutrient and that my timing is perfect and elegant.

My deepest gratitude to my husband DAN, whose blue eyes twinkle every time I say: "I have an idea!" Thank you for your fortitude, patience, calmness, and for being the best papa bear ever to our B. And we'll always have Paris.

Thank you to my bestie ALICIA GLASSBURN BILIOURIS – watching our lives unfold has been magical.

Thank you to my mama bird and mother, BARBARA SCHAAF MERRILL, for her strength, creativity, musicality, and love, and to raise me to have grit and to be a free thinker.

Thank you to my sister, MARLENE A. MERRILL, whose tenacity and quest for excellent is unparalleled and an inspiration.

Thank you to DR. MARION REID, whose deep friendship and genius reminds me that if you love what you do, it's not work (so true!).

And a deep thank you to designer extraordinaire CHRISTY JENKINS, who patiently helped turn my concepts into such a thing of beauty.

With love and appreciation – M.M.T.

Let us be grateful to people who make us happy. They are the charming gardeners who make our souls blossom.
— MARCEL PROUST

About Marianne Merritt Talbot

Marianne is an attorney, writer, coach, entrepreneur, former law professor, former AmLaw 100 business development professional, and mom. A born and bred New York City kid with dreams of becoming a violinist – or a civil rights attorney – Marianne learned early on how to develop creativity and cultivate hustle. In college, Marianne was a Women's Studies major, including teaching "Introduction to Feminism" classes to undergraduates and leading numerous feminist initiatives. In law school, Marianne was a law clerk at leading civil rights organizations, including at the NAACP Legal Defense and Educational Fund, the Lawyers' Committee for Civil Rights Under Law, and the United States Department of Justice, Civil Rights Division.

As a trial attorney, Marianne handled complex civil litigation and civil rights matters in New York, Washington D.C., and Virginia, in majority part as the protégé of Philip J. Hirschkop, one of the legendary lawyers who won the landmark case of *Loving v. Virginia* before the Supreme Court of the United States. She also was an adjunct law professor at the American University, Washington College of Law and the George Washington University Law School. She has written and spoken widely on many business and legal topics, and has delivered numerous CLE programs on numerous topics, including business development.

After litigating for 14 years, Marianne retired and founded her own coaching and training firm in Manhattan, where she worked with an amazing roster of clients, including an award-winning actress, Madison Avenue designer, and a multitude of high-performing professionals in the fields of law, tech, finance, and the arts. Marianne now dedicates her professional life to working with attorneys in many capacities, including training, coaching, and designing diversity initiatives. She particularly loves working with women attorneys – helping them strategize their careers, build books of business, and, most importantly, create lives of prosperity, joy, love, and pleasure.

Marianne currently lives in the Washington, D.C. area with her husband Daniel and beautiful daughter Barbara. Her approach to life is embodied in the iconic quote by Ralph Waldo Emerson:

> *Nothing great was ever created without enthusiasm.*

www.ingramcontent.com/pod-product-compliance
Lightning Source LLC
Chambersburg PA
CBHW042035100526
44587CB00030B/4427